SODOM
IN
AMERICA

A Candid Biblical View
of
Homosexuality

RICHARD SONES

CONTENTS

FOREWORD

In order to come to any Christian understanding of the issues that present themselves and vie for acceptance on the social and political stage, it is paramount to accept the authority of the Bible and to understand what it teaches.

The Bible is a collection of 66 books and letters written by many authors over several millennia. The various books and letters were also written in different languages; Hebrew, Aramaic, and Greek. The consensus of biblical scholarship agrees that Job was the first book written, while the writings of John are the most recent.

The Bible comes to us through many means. The books attributed to Moses were probably first passed from generation to generation orally. By the 15th century modern printing presses with movable type were used to print books such as the Gutenberg Bible, a Latin translation printed in Germany. Prior to that, all books and letters were copied by hand.

Those in antiquity responsible for copying the Old Testament had a reverence for the text that resulted in incredibly accurate copies. After a copy was made, they counted the letters to make sure the copy was exact. The tick marks used in counting have been preserved along with the text. At the end of their useful life, copies of Old Testament books were buried in Bible cemeteries available for archeologists to find centuries later. The same regard was not given to New Testament texts, so there are quite a few spelling mistakes and other minor variations from copy to copy. All in all, the Bible is the most researched and studied book from an archeological and literary perspective of any work in all of history.

Some people have a hard time trusting the Bible because they contend it was written by men and no man is good or perfect enough to author the words of God. Such reasoning precludes the possibility of the Bible existing. But if God is indeed all powerful and all knowing, He should be able to figure out a way to make it possible.

A deacon in a small country church in rural Virginia gave the new young pastor some chickens to put in the chicken house behind the parsonage. One day, one of the chickens got out of the house. The pastor chased the chicken around the yard and toward the door of the coop, but every time the chicken got near the door, it would sharply turn and run off in another direction.

The chase went on for some time until the pastor suddenly got an idea. He promptly stopped chasing the chicken and walked back into the house. Moments later, he came out with the feed bag and walked directly to the chicken house making noise by shaking the bag but ignoring the wayward chicken. The chicken stopped running away and followed the pastor into the chicken house.

The pastor was able to get the chicken to do his bidding without being able to speak chicken. But the feed bag was something the chicken understood. The young minister got the chicken to want to return to the safety of the coop using the only means of communication available. Man is significantly smarter than a chicken.

How much smarter than man is God? The question should not be, "Is man capable of writing the Bible?" For the answer to that question is certainly, "No." But to the question, "Is God capable of communicating in writing with man?" If God is God, then the answer is decisively "Yes."

Keeping with the example, the young pastor was not trying to communicate that it was time to eat. He was trying to get the chicken inside the coop, safely locked away from prowling foxes. The feed bag was successful because chickens are always ready to eat. There's no way to know if the chicken ever appreciated the end result.

Sometimes the words of the Bible alone are incapable of communicating what we need to know. In John 3, for example, Jesus tells Nicodemus that the only way anyone can see the kingdom of God is to be born again. At face value, we are as confused as Nicodemus was when Jesus told him. In such instances, the Spirit of God is able to communicate truth to our spirit through the words of scripture. Our mind has to catch up in those instances.

To gain a true understanding of scripture it is essential that passages are taken in context. Taking a passage out of context can lead to a complete misunderstanding of the point and meaning of the passage.

Consider the preacher who bragged that he could preach a powerful sermon on any scripture. One of his hearers shouted out, "Oh yeah? How about, 'These eight did milk a bear.'" The preacher thought a moment, and then began his sermon talking about the courage and teamwork these eight must have had. He bellowed on about the enormity of the task they had undertaken and the extent of their bravery. He was interrupted and shown the passage in context.

The final paragraph in Genesis 22 in the American Standard Version (1901) states: "And it came to pass after these things that it was told Abraham, saying, behold Milcah, she also hath born children unto thy brother Nahor. Uz his first born, and Buz his brother, and Kemuel the father of Aram. And Chesed and Hazo, and Pildash, and Jidlaph, and Bethuel. And Bethuel begat Rebekah. **These eight did Milcah bear** to Nahor, Abraham's brother. And his concubine, whose name was Reumah, she also bare Tebah, and Gaham, and Tahash, and Maacah."

Those outside the Christian faith reject any authority of the Bible. Some go so far as to call the Bible a collection of myths or fairy tales. No matter how difficult or easy to understand, however, accepting the Bible as the Word of God requires faith.

"The world has no motivation to hate you, but hates me because I expose its evil undertakings."

Jesus – John 7:7

INTRODUCTION

The Role Of Fear In Christian Attitudes

Fear is something that Christians have dealt with since the time of Christ. Hebrews 2 points out that one of the reasons Jesus died for us was to enable us to overcome fear.

Fear is the strongest human emotion. It will take hold and replace any other feeling in a heartbeat. A young couple in love and enchanted with each other will lose all the mushy feelings when the slightest threat to their romance is revealed. Even anger is not as strong as fear. A sudden loud, crashing noise or the announcement of imminent disaster will cause most anyone to lose whatever train of thought they were pursuing.

Fear is irrational. Its effects are felt whether it has any basis in reality or not. Consider Fred, for instance, the employee of a company that was cutting back on expenses. One day a close coworker rushed into his office and told him, "I just overheard the boss mention your name as a possible lay-off candidate." It would be perfectly natural for Fred's heart to sink, for him to drop whatever he was working on so as to get a resume ready and begin the search for a new job. Fear naturally sets in. But suppose this co-worker was in the habit of playing practical jokes to get a rise out of Fred in one way or another and Fred just had a very good meeting with the boss in which he showered him with accolades. In that case, when his coworker rushes in and tells him, "I just overheard the boss mention your name as a possible lay-off candidate," Fred may fake a reaction of terror before laughing out loud at him. Fear won't set in; the joke was on the prankster.

The difference in whether or not someone experiences fear does not lie in the message being delivered, but in whether they believe it or not. In fact, the coworker in the previous example was not playing a joke on Fred; he really did hear what he said he heard and now finds himself in the position of the fabled boy who cried wolf, trying to convince his friend of his sincerity. The boss was in fact being nice to Fred to soften the blow since he had no choice but to lay him off. The difference in whether or not someone experiences fear is not based on the truth of the message, but whether the message is believed. If Fred believed he was threatened, he would naturally feel fear, regardless of whether he was truly being threatened.

Fear works the same way for everyone. It is a result of the beliefs that are conjured up in the mind, loosely tied to the perception of the present and the experiences of the past.

All fear is ultimately rooted in the fear of death. Fear, on the surface, may seem that it is only related to loss, but if the loss were not perceived as insurmountable, there would be no fear involved. The prospect of a million dollar law suit to a billionaire, while not preferable, could be taken in stride. But the prospect of a million dollar law suit to someone with humble means living from paycheck to paycheck would provoke fear to the point of panic. The fear they experience is indirectly the fear of death. It is not outright and certainly not obvious, but rises out of the illusory culmination of events; lose in court, can't pay, lose all possessions, spend rest of life in prison, die.

Even the smallest fears are, in due course, rooted in death. He missed a deadline at work and can't let anyone know or the boss will fire him. He'll lose his reputation and all his friends. Then he won't be able to get another job and have to sell everything he owns to survive. Finally, he'll run out of money and starve to death.

Fear can only survive in the absence of faith. Fear might well be called the opposite of faith. Where faith is assurance, fear is the lack of assurance. Where faith is evidence, fear is the unknown.

It's important to have the correct perspective to understand the relationship between a Christian and God. Everything about the relationship is for the benefit of the Christian. God is completely self-sufficient. He does not need man, the world, or anything in it at all. He does not need to be defended by man, as if that were even possible. He has our devotion and faith because He is God, not because He needs our devotion or faith. God is not God by popular vote or because anyone believes in Him or needs Him. When this world with all that inhabit it gasps its last breath and passes away, God will still be God.

Beginning with Abraham, we learned that God loves us and wants to help us. Mankind was the culminating act of His creation. Every direction He has given us is for our own good and for the good of those whose lives we may affect. His laws are meant to protect us, especially from things we can't see, don't know about, or don't understand, similar to the way a parent tries to protect a toddler from a hot stove or electric outlet.

All people have the freedom to choose to listen and obey God or to ignore Him and go their own way. Choosing to obey leads to faith; choosing to ignore leads to fear. Ultimately, God promised a reward for those who follow Him and destruction for those who turn away.

God expects His followers to reach out and help those around them just as He reached out to Abraham. In order to help His people do that, He promised to take care of them, even in death. His promises are meant to dispel the fears of His people. Everything on the devil's "what if" list is on God's "I can take care of" list.

One significant and troubling characteristic of man is his tendency to think of himself as a god. Although very few people throughout history have gone so far as to publically claim to be a god, man is uncomfortable unless he has everything figured out and under control. This results in men working to the point in which they believe they understand what God wants, and then marching ahead through the specifics without talking to God. It's all too common for Christians to receive the initial instruction from God and respond, "Thanks God; I'll take it from here." On the other hand, acting on faith with nothing more than the leading and assurance of God can be terrifying.

The difficulties in life provide ample opportunities for fear. Pat answers are rarely sufficient to deal with the real problems of life. Let's say a child contracts a rare and strange disease and winds up unconscious, in critical condition in a hospital. A Christian is called to come pray for the child. How should he pray? He knows from 1st John that God answers prayers according to His wishes. So the real question is: what does God want in this circumstance? Is the child suffering from a sickness leading to death or is it an occasion for God to display His power? (John 11:4) Hopefully, and for the sake of the child and family, fear and the theology of the person praying won't get in the way of what God's wishes are in that specific circumstance.

God intended for the Christian to be free of fear. He did everything possible to make that happen, but boldness comes only with faith.

There are a number of common fears that inhibit a person's faith, and as a consequence, hinder his ability to meet other people's needs in the way God intended. All of those fears arise out of the person's thinking of themselves. Public speaking, for instance, can be a harrowing experience. Standing in front of a group of people as the center of attention can be terrifying. If a speaker is focused on the importance of the message and the criticality of the hearers getting it right, there is less chance of anxious feelings than if the speaker is worried about what he looks like, sounds like, or what the others are thinking about him.

A major source of fear for the Christian is the worry about other people's opinions. Perhaps the biggest fear in this category is the fear of being different. No one enjoys being separated out from the crowd. Standing out invites extra attention and scrutiny. It opens the possibility that one's darkest secrets will be exposed or some hidden flaw will become known. Fear drives people to blend in with the crowd. For the Christian, that means it's all right to help people but only in approved ways. In that case, it's not God's approval, but family, friends, neighbors and possibly casual acquaintances whose opinion is most valued.

Another fear in the people's opinion category is the fear of looking stupid. Society has gone to great lengths to make sure that people know what they're doing before they try to help others. In today's world you can't even cut someone's hair without a license. If a Christian tries to help somebody, they run the risk of being judged an amateur or being criticized for not doing it right or leaving something out. The same fear underpins the false perception that ministry should only be carried out by trained professionals.

But God places no value at all on the opinions of men. He deals with individuals directly, one on one, without regard to what anyone else may do or think. In order for Christians to grow spiritually, be obedient and effective, they must prayerfully take direction from God. It helps immensely to have a working knowledge of the Bible, on the other hand traditions, specific denominational teachings, and the advice and opinions of family and friends could prove to be stumbling blocks.

Attitude is the way a person thinks about something or someone. If a Christian is influenced by fear, it will shape his attitude toward others. Fear always considers self-preservation paramount. An attitude molded by fears will keep the Christian on the defensive. That attitude perverts the understanding of what's happening in ministry, like the speechmaker worried about what he looks or sounds like.

A Christian's attitudes become apparent through his actions. Christ-like behavior flows from having a Christ-like outlook. That involves honestly admitting that God knows more and He alone has it all figured out. It comes from not worrying about what other people think or their opinions. Probably most importantly, it comes from resting in the faith that God knows what He's asking and will protect those who obey Him.

In 1Timothy 2, Paul tells us we shouldn't be afraid to tell others about Jesus because God has given us a spirit of power and love and discipline.

Focusing on the hurts and needs of others brings out the power, love, and discipline from the Spirit of God within.

Jesus said that it was irrational to fear men who are only capable of posing a temporal threat instead of God who can threaten presently and eternally. About half a dozen times in scripture it teaches that the beginning of wisdom is the fear of the Lord. Fear of the Lord means first of all believing that the Lord is. Fear of the Lord also means believing His word. Lastly, it means obeying His words.

The Role Of Prejudice In Christian Attitudes

During the ethnic civil war in former Yugoslavia, a young Croatian Christian was asked why they were fighting the Bosnians. The war hardened young woman who looked to be no more than twenty-five responded, "They go to different churches. They dress differently than us." And for that, they were willing to kill each other.

Atheists are happy to point out that, throughout history, more people have been killed in the cause of organized religion than for any other reason. The root cause of much of that killing is prejudice and the resulting false assumptions.

Prejudice is, basically, judging individuals before knowing them. It is the practice of generalizing a group of people from the experience or reputation of a particular person. It believes that every member of the group is or acts in a certain way because one or even most of the group is perceived as such. It is the aggregate of assumptions made about a person based on some outward, usually unrelated, appearance or action. The assumptions are invariably incorrect. Prejudice leads to unfair treatment, hurt feelings, anger, and resentment. It is also a guaranteed way to destroy relationships, cripple a church and quash ministry. As seekers of the truth, Christians should do all that is in their power to avoid prejudice.

The most widely known and celebrated basis of prejudice in America is skin color. At a Christian pastors' conference many years ago, a dark skinned minister made a remark to a light skinned minister, "Your ancestors kept my ancestors as slaves." That is a classic example of racial prejudice. The false assumptions being that all light skinned people are descended from wealthy slave owning families originating in the south-east portion of the country. This particular light skinned pastor was, in fact, the son of a European immigrant and a very poor American family. With no connection at all to the slavery issue, he was at a total loss concerning how to respond, except in anger and resentment.

While it is undeniable that slavery existed and predominately true that light skinned individuals living in the Old South bought and used dark skinned individuals, it is wrong to assume that all light skinned individuals owned all dark skinned individuals. Much, if not all prejudice is the result of emotional reaction and not sound logic.

Prejudice can be based on many things including religion, a major root of prejudice. Catholics and Protestants in Europe fought major wars that lasted decades, almost from the start of the protestant reformation. In the name of Christianity, they decimated their homeland. Religious prejudice is usually based on very little actual knowledge about the religion. In the first century, part of the reason Christianity was against Roman law was that the Romans widely believed the Christians practiced cannibalism. Outsiders got wind of the ritual of eating the body of Christ during the Lord's Supper and subsequently spread false rumors.

The somber and spiritually sobering truth is that no Christian denomination is absolutely correct in its doctrine. The fact that God wants Christians to live by faith in Christ means that He never intended for everything to be spelled out. That is not to say that we can't know anything, but prejudice takes a little knowledge and distorts it with a lot of conjecture.

Prejudice can also be based on a person's clothing, how they wear their hair, what kind of car they drive, for whom they voted, and the list goes on. The hurtful suppositions derived from someone's outward appearance usually involve beliefs, attitudes, character, values, personalities and other unseen qualities that can't possibly be known by merely looking at someone or by knowing some isolated tidbit of information.

Prejudice is dangerous because it is a common human weakness interrelated with the way we gain understanding. Learning comes through experience, and it is only natural for people to translate their past experiences into relevant present knowledge. That works pretty well for figuring out nature and inanimate objects, but no two people are the same. Unpleasant experiences with three successive cab drivers will not yield any information about the abilities or personality of the next cab driver, though naturally, we make assumptions which easily lead to false beliefs on our part.

Prejudice leads to mistrust and sometimes misplaced trust. Americans are learning every day that a book shouldn't be judged by its cover, even when the cover looks great. Government officials at every level have been exposed from time to time as being dishonest, corrupt, self-seeking, and profiteering. The reason such people make big headlines when they are caught is that they have abused the public trust. The same grounds for prejudice also work regarding misplaced trust. It's very easy to trust a well-groomed, attractive, fancy car driving, sometimes robe and a clerical collar wearing person. Prejudice can get a person in trouble. Case in point, con artists count on prejudice in order to be able to make their schemes work.

Perhaps the most dangerous consequence of prejudice for the Christian and for the church is the tendency to allow prejudicial thoughts and attitudes to redefine one's theology. Whenever human reasoning is used to understand the things of God, it must be constrained by what is taught in scripture. To attempt to justify prejudice by disproving something in scripture by using other scripture is pure folly.

The effects of early, theologically based,

prejudice in American history were far reaching and devastating. When the Europeans first discovered the Americas and began to colonize, they discovered indigenous peoples already inhabiting the lands. Popular European theology reasoned that since the gospel had already been proclaimed to all men, these newly discovered creatures were not really human, but somehow substandard and without souls. Centuries later, when men were imported from Africa as a cheap labor source, the same theologically based rationale led to their mistreatment.

It is impossible for Christians to follow God if they have rewritten God's directions in their minds. Those who attempt to do so are in reality following their separate ways. Since that happens so easily and naturally, it's vital for all Christians to be open and honest with God about the circumstances in which they find themselves and His direction concerning them.

Confusion on What the Bible Says about Homosexuality

Homosexuality is not new. The practice has been around for thousands of years. The Bible addresses the practice frankly but also gives a perspective as to God's motives that form the foundation of His guiding principles.

Since homosexual "Rights" have come to the forefront of politics worldwide, much has appeared or been heard in public concerning what the Bible says on the topic. Individuals, pro and con, on the political aspects of the subject have been guilty of proof-texting. Proof-texting from the Bible happens when a particular set of words are taken out of context and used to convey something other than what the text expresses. Occasionally, mistranslations or misinterpretations are also sensationalized in popular media.

Many Christians have never seriously studied the subject from the scriptures and are therefore in danger of believing the volume of prevalent false teachings.

This book will examine in depth the topic of homosexuality as discussed in the Bible.

"You can count on this fact and unconditionally believe that Jesus Christ came into this world to save wicked men, among whom I am number one."

Paul – 1st Timothy 1:15

SIN

A Sin is a Sin

Sin, as most commonly used in the Bible, means to miss the mark or fall short of God's expectation. In the gospels, the same concept is applied in such a way that common people were referred to as sinners. Jesus understood that everyone misses the mark God sets for them. The majority of people sin due to their inability to be perfect rather than out of premeditation. Paul made it clear in the book of Romans that all men fall short of God's expectations. Christians tend to ignore the universal aspect of sin when they think about it. By focusing on what is perceived to be heinous sins, they subconsciously place themselves in the judge's seat, unwittingly earning a harsher judgment from God.

Sin, however, is also defined as the intentional rebellion, offenses and violations of the law that men carry out. From the day Cain killed his brother, Abel, in a jealous rage, men have allowed themselves to be carried away by their own emotions and aspirations and acted accordingly. Fear, jealousy, lust, and greed are among the many powerful motivators to willingly and intentionally commit sin. The decision to sin intentionally happens in the moment that even Christians tell themselves that God doesn't care or that God's not paying attention.

Slowly, over the years, Americans have come to equate right and wrong with legal and illegal. When the country was founded, legal and illegal corresponded closely in practice with Biblical guidance, though not often expressly attributed. The subtle change in the authority for right and wrong has taken place almost imperceptibly to the average American. For decades, godless men and women have worked hard to replace the God of the Bible with the god of their own imagination. The spiritual battle, however, has never been in the political or legal arena. That battle has always been in the hearts of individuals. God knows it, and man's spiritual adversary knows it.

When in the mid-sixties, prominent atheist Madeline Murray O'Hare, seeking to abolish prayer in public schools, brought a lawsuit on behalf of her son, she quietly encouraged two beliefs that are widely accepted today by Americans. First, right and wrong are based on law, and second, the U.S. Constitution is god.

We cannot use the system of law worked out by our government to understand how God judges sin. Our system of laws grades the importance of a law by the severity of the consequences for breaking it. If the impatient speed down the highway, they will have to mail in a fine if they are stopped at all. If they rob a bank, they will spend some time locked away. If they maliciously plan and then kill several people, they are probably going to pay with their own life. The relative importance of God's laws depends on the source of the law. Since He is the source of all His laws, all are equally important.

Sin is an act of the heart which may not necessarily be carried out physically. Case in point, Jesus revealed that God regards anger in the same light and just as serious as murder. Unloving, hostile attitudes and actions of the heart separate a man from God whether he crosses the line and takes physical action or not.

James explains in his second chapter that a person who only commits one sin is guilty of breaking all of God's law. One false accusation against someone carries the same judgment and penalty as murder. So for the purpose of justification before God, every sin is equal, whether it is the result of the vilest kind of hatred or a careless act of selfishness.

God arranged a way for men to receive a pardon by having Jesus take the blame for their sin when He died on the cross. Individuals are pardoned by God on the basis of their faith in Christ and the obedience that flows from their faith. Obedience is not a one-time deed, but a pattern of submission that begins with repentance and develops throughout life.

Due to the death and resurrection of Jesus, there have only been two kinds of people in the world: justified and unjustified. The justified are spiritually alive, selfless and spread life. The unjustified are spiritually dead, selfish, and focused only on themselves. The number and type of specific sins they have committed is irrelevant in either case. The justified have all their sins forgiven. The unjustified are condemned even if they have only committed a single sin.

The Ten Commandments

As a brand new fledgling nation just freed from Egyptian slavery, the descendants of Israel gathered at the base of what became known as the mountain of God where Moses received detailed instructions on how to proceed. Most notably, he received the two stone tablets on which were written the Ten Commandments.

Of the more than six hundred laws that Moses passed on to the people, the Ten Commandments are regarded as the major laws. God told Moses that these commandments were Israel's part of the treaty that He was making with them. As long as the people kept the treaty, He would protect them, heal them, and be their God.

The first five commandments have to do with man's relationship to God.

After taking credit for their dramatic rescue from Egypt, one of the world's most powerful nations at that time, God demanded plainly that they not turn to any other god.

Though on the surface seemingly irrelevant today, the second commandment is, to be sure, enormously important. It is a prohibition against making, having, or serving idols. It carries with it a curse on the violator's children, grandchildren, and great grandchildren. The second commandment goes hand in hand with the first. Don't turn to any other god and don't make any gods for yourself.

To understand the importance of the second commandment and the significance of the curse, it helps to understand the principle of authority.

Authority flows from God and through Jesus according to Matthew, chapter 28. Authority carries with it the responsibility for selfless love. John proclaims that God is love and thereby demonstrates His authority. At the bottom of the line of authority are the angels which are described as being created a little higher than man. They are also described as being ever present before God and always obedient.

The commandment against idolatry was meant to protect man spiritually. As the creator, God jealously guards His creation. Any other god man turns to is either the competition or a sham. If the god is a sham, in other words not a god at all, then a man who follows it is unprotected. If a man turns to the enemy of God, he will be destroyed presently and forever. A protracted example of the principle of authority and the protection it offers is found in the book of Job.

Job was a Godly man to the extent that God bragged on him to Satan. Satan suggested that Job's righteousness was due to God's protection and blessing. By the conclusion of the book it is plain to see that God's protection and Job's blessings were due to his righteousness, and not the other way around.

The second commandment warns that

violators will have their children punished. That is because idolatry creates a weakness in the parents that is passed on to the children and easily exploited by the enemy in their lives. This principle is so obvious that scientists have started to look for genes to explain the seeming heredity nature of sin. In fact, a solitary righteous, God fearing person in the chain can break the curse for himself and his children.

The first defeat the nation of Israel suffered after they crossed the Jordan River into the Promised Land was on account of idolatry. From that ill-fated beginning and throughout their history, Israel struggled with idolatry, particularly with Baal, the Ashtoreth, and the gods of the neighboring nations. At times, even the king gave in to practicing idolatry. Idolatry is the first step away from God. It is the first, "Thou shalt not" commandment and the only one that uses the prohibitive phrase twice.

The third commandment has to do with God's name which He protects as well as His people. Hypocritically using the name of God dilutes His name.

Jesus told the Pharisees that God created the Sabbath for man. The law to observe the Sabbath was not a forced day off, but a way for God to show His people that He was able to take care of them while they rested. In addition to the Sabbath day established in the Ten Commandments, there was also a Sabbath year every seven years.

The fifth commandment, to honor father and mother, is the only commandment with a promise of blessing. Parents stand in the place of God for their young children. When children honor their parents, they honor God. Godly parents, by their actions and character, convey to a child the invisible attributes of God. That is why child abuse is not only illegal, it is a sin against the nature of God. At the same time, parents learn a great deal about God's perspective in their dealings with their children.

Good parents will love their children unconditionally. No one will blame or look down on the parents who love and stand by their son or daughter, no matter how heinous the crime the child may have committed. Even when discipline is required, the love of a parent can come through in such a way that the child can understand the unconditional love God has for them.

Conversely, God promises in several passages of scripture to extinguish the light of the person who does not honor his parents. God protects His name, His people, and His character.

The remaining five commandments have to do with man's relationship to his fellow man.

The sixth commandment prohibits murder. The Aramaic is straightforward and simply says, "No murder!" The Aramaic word, "*Ratsach*" which is translated as "kill" in some translations and "murder" in others, means to murder a person and is used only in that context. The law spelled out that the penalty for murder was death. The scripture clearly explains the process for determining the person, called the avenger of blood, responsible for carrying out the execution. The commandment did not apply to accidents. The murder had to be intentional, premeditated, and verified by multiple witnesses. Refuge cities were established to assure the accused murderer got a fair trial by the congregation.

The seventh commandment prohibits adultery. Adultery occurs when a married person has sex with someone other than his or her spouse.

The eighth commandment prohibits stealing. Stealing occurs when someone takes something without permission that doesn't belong to him.

The ninth commandment prohibits false testimony against someone else. A law given in Leviticus tells the people to refrain from dealing falsely with each other and refrain from lying to each other. Lying is not a part of the nature or character of God. The Old and New Testaments both declare that God is incapable of lying. Lying is often motivated by fear and will slowly destroy relationships.

Only God knows if a person has broken the tenth commandment. It addresses certain actions of the heart. The last commandment Moses brought down from the mountain prohibited coveting. To covet simply means to want something that belongs to someone else. Coveting is dangerous because it inspires feelings that, when acted on, break other commandments such as stealing, adultery, and murder. Coveting property, relationships, animals, or anything else someone else had was prohibited.

The Tutor

Relating to God and our fellow man does not come naturally for anyone due to fear and selfishness. At the time God tapped Abraham on the shoulder and said He wanted to be friends, the prevailing belief in the world about divine beings provoked even more fear. In his day, gods were looked upon as uncaring malevolent beings that used men for sport and entertainment and were to be avoided if at all possible.

When God Most High revealed Himself to Abraham as a purposeful and loving God, Abraham needed more than just a shift in thinking. Everything was new and surprising. The gods that man had conceived were nothing like the real God, who from the beginning communicated His desire to have a people that would follow and honor Him.

The solemn agreement that God made with His people under Moses was a covenant of laws. The fledgling nation of Israel had grown up with little guidance from God. The experience and teachings handed down from the patriarchs were not sufficient to guide the nation. After Moses gave the people God's laws, he told them of the many blessings that would follow them if they obeyed. Conversely, all those blessings would turn to curses if they disobeyed, with a special punishment reserved for those who willfully and knowingly lived in rebellion against God.

God taught His people through His law how to relate to one another and how to honor Him. But as the New Testament points out in several places, their fear and selfishness were too great an influence for them to overcome. In Jeremiah, chapter 31, God revealed to the prophet that He was going to make a new covenant with His people that would be different from the one they broke. He said He would put His law inside them and write it on their hearts.

In the meantime, the written law served as a teacher, a protector, and a guide for God's people. Seemingly insignificant details drilled into the minds of the young nation of Israel foretold events that were yet to come and painted a picture of the future messiah. Had the student nation learned its lesson, Christ would have been readily recognized and understood. But even in Jesus' day and in the presence of His miraculous deeds, pride and selfish ambition blinded those who should have been the first to recognize and follow Him.

The law still functions as a tutor for those who do not know God. And for those who live their lives according to their own standard, the law points out what is sin. God's law, for example, says, "Do not murder." Even if a federal or state law is passed that makes murder legal, the most hardened and self-reliant atheist will know that murder is sin. They may not believe it or agree with it, but they will know it.

To be an effective teacher, the law can make no exceptions. It is unrelenting and unforgiving, and according to the law, ignorance is no excuse. God's law in that respect is just like natural laws. If anyone is ignorant of the law of gravity and steps off the side of a bridge, the inevitable fall and landing in the water will hopefully teach something about that specific law. People all over the world lived under and instinctively knew about the law of gravity long before Isaac Newton gave it a name. All of God's laws are just as sure and immutable.

Jesus simplifies the law, summing it up into a memorable principle in a couple of places. Mathew, chapter seven, is mainly focused on hypocrisy. In these verses, He said the golden rule sums up the law and the prophets. Do for others the things you want others to do for you. Later, in chapter 22, a lawyer asked Jesus what the greatest commandment was. He replied that the greatest commandment was to love God with all your being. He also said the second greatest and similar commandment was to love others as one's self. He added that all of the other laws and the teaching of the prophets were based on these two. It's interesting that both these chapters include a discussion of getting into and being shut out of heaven.

Sin, in a nutshell, can be thought of as dishonoring God. It is selfishness to the point of mistreating someone else. An evil person will sin knowingly, willfully, and intentionally. But everyone gives in to their own nature now and then and misbehaves unintentionally and carelessly. The law was given to man to help him understand specifically what sin looked like and how to avoid it.

The Other Side of Sin

Sin is the main problem that all of humanity faces. God either deals with sin by judgment or through forgiveness. All sin is penalized, and according to scripture, the penalty is death. The only question is who pays the penalty. For the believers and followers of Christ, the liability of their sin was recompensed on the cross making God's forgiveness of the believer possible. For those who do not know God, they will pay the penalty with their own lives.

Forgiveness comes with a stipulation that Jesus made clear on more than one occasion. For example, in Matthew 6 Jesus is teaching His followers to avoid the practices of hypocrites. Phony pretenders show off and do what appears to be good so that others will see them and think highly of them. God sees in the secret and hidden places of the heart and knows a man's motivations and if he is sincere.

In the course of that teaching He gives what has become known as the Lord's Prayer, but it is really an example for disciples to follow when they shut themselves up in their quiet place and pray. During the course of the prayer He teaches, "Forgive us our debts\sins\trespasses as we forgive our debtors\those who sin\trespass against us." In the two verses after the conclusion of the prayer He adds the condition of forgiveness. Verse 14 says that if anyone forgives an individual who has sinned against him, then God will forgive that person. Verse 15 says that if anyone refuses to forgive those who have wronged him, God will withhold forgiveness from that person as well. Thus it is stated in three separate ways that our forgiveness is contingent on our being willing to forgive.

Jesus also made it clear to His disciples that God expects His people to be a forgiving people. The average person with average patience is reluctant to forgive someone after he has wronged him in the same way two or three times. In Matthew, chapter 18, Peter alluded to that when he asked Jesus to tell him how many times he should forgive someone. Peter thought seven times was plenty, but Jesus told him 490 times. Then Jesus told Peter this parable to explain how God dealt with sin.

A king, during the course of settling accounts, had one of his servants brought in who had borrowed about a hundred pounds of silver and was unable to repay the debt. The servant fell to the ground and begged for more time promising that he would repay every penny he owed. The king felt sorry for him and told him to forget about the debt.

For unexplained reasons, the forgiven servant later found a fellow servant who owed him a little less than fourteen ounces of silver. He grabbed him by the throat and demanded to be paid. His fellow servant pleaded for a little time and promised to repay what he owed. But the man refused and had his comrade thrown into prison.

When the king got word of what had happened, he arrested the man and held a summary court hearing demanding to know why the man failed to show even in a small measure the compassion that had been shown to him. The king called him a wicked man and handed him over to be tortured until he paid the 100 pounds of silver that he owed.

We see by his actions that the king expected the forgiven servant to pass on less than one percent of the hundred pounds of silver he had just collected to his fellow servant.

The chapter ends with Jesus' warning that God will do the same to those who refuse to forgive with their whole heart. Jesus wanted Peter to understand that the wrongs committed against him were trivial in comparison to his sin against God, and if God was willing to forgive, then Peter should be willing to forgive as well.

Jesus also showed by example how a Christian should deal with sin, even sexual sins. One day while He was teaching a crowd of people in the temple, a group of lawyers and religious elders interrupted Him. They dragged a woman along and sat her in front of Him and told Him that she had been caught committing adultery. They emphasized that she had been caught in the act, which means that whoever caught her busted in while she and her lover were having sex. Perhaps her husband came home early from work, discovered her in flagrante delicto, and then reported her to the authorities. The passage doesn't say.

They knew the letter of the law better than anyone and asked Jesus if they should follow the law which dictated in this case that she was to be executed by stoning. No one will ever know this side of heaven what the words were that Jesus wrote in the dirt in response to their question, but they continued to press Him for an answer. With the wisdom of Solomon he told them to follow the law and stone her to death. He asked the one who had never sinned to throw the first stone.

When the crowd and the accusers had all left, He told the woman that He forgave her, and He counseled her to sin no more. His response and the way that He handled her sin angered the self-righteous "followers of the law" but brought healing and life to the woman and most likely her friends and those close to her.

In this example, just as in His teaching, Jesus reminds the accusers of their own sin. Perhaps He wrote laws in the dirt such as "Honor your father and mother," "Do not lie," "Do not covet." Whatever it was, the elders among the accusers got the message and could not oppose Him from a standpoint of righteousness. Jesus knew the law too.

How often do we bring our grievances to Jesus and ask Him to throw the first stone. But God's ways never change, and we, like Peter, are charged to forgive lest we forfeit our own forgiveness.

Near the end of the 6th century, Pope Gregory wrote a list of seven deadly sins which was made famous almost a millennium later by Dante Alighiere's work, *The Divine Comedy*.

Like the Apostle John's summation of all that is in the world, the seven deadly sins are common motivations behind sin. They may be thought of as the pesky sins that the book of Hebrews warns us to avoid using the analogy of a runner who sheds unnecessary things that weigh him down in a race. Pope Gregory listed Pride, Lust, Avarice, Gluttony, Anger, Envy, and Sloth. It is within human nature to struggle with at least one of these. It is unlikely that anyone would be tempted by all seven and since everyone is different, each will have his own individual weakness. The Apostle Paul identified his struggle with envy. As John said, if a man denies he has sin he is a blatant liar.

Most of the sins on the list can't be seen. They

are attitudes of the heart which prompt the acts of sin committed against God and others. Failure to forgive another's sin is the height of hypocrisy.

Pride is an attitude of self-importance or self-worth in worldly terms. Proverbs 16 cautions that pride leads to a falling down and destruction. The danger in pride is twofold. First, like Lucifer, a proud person becomes his own god and ignores the leading of God. In addition, pride leads to an attitude of contempt for other people making it impossible to relate to them in a Christ-like manner. Pride stems from an out of proportion need for self-worth or a good self-image.

The opposite of pride is humility. Romans 12 instructs plainly that a Christian should honestly appraise himself and not think more highly of himself than he should. Humility is not necessarily meekness, but an attitude derived from the honest assessment and understanding of one's strengths and limitations. In Numbers 12 Moses is described as the most humble man on earth, yet he was confident and powerful enough to lead a nation in battle. James ties the two together when he refers to Proverbs 3, cautioning us that God opposes those who are proud but shows His favor to those who are humble.

Lust is the hunger for things. John breaks lust down to the lust of the world and the lust of the eyes. Lust passes as need, for example, the need of a new car or the need for prettier clothes. Effective marketing techniques hinge on a person's lust. The lust of the eyes is the desire to see; to see what's next, or to see what's hidden, for instance. A sure way to fire up a person's curiosity and desire to see something is to tell them to not look as God told Lot and his family as he escorted them out of Sodom. Lot's wife couldn't resist the temptation to peek. The principle behind the success of a soap opera is the hook set in the closing minutes. Viewers tune in for the next installment because they have to know what happens next.

When an individual's wants are stronger than his patience for God to meet his genuine needs, lust is the result. David expressed his commitment to avoid just that in the first verse of the 23rd psalm.

The opposite of lust is contentment. God always meets the needs of His people just as He promised. There is a certain peace that comes with contentment that lust tries to take away. Paul frequently found himself in disconcerting circumstances, yet he told the Philippians that the reason he never troubled them with his needs is that he had learned to be content in whatever situation in which he found himself. He also instructed Timothy to be content with food and clothing. Being content is a decision that anyone can choose to make at any time.

Avarice is another word for greed. Greed is the hording of things, especially money. Jesus teaches over and over that our lives are not equal to our possessions. Greed is dangerous because it fosters a mistrust of God. All we have is from God and given to us for a purpose. Greed forgets that purpose and promotes the lie that we are in control and what we have is ours. Greed is born out of insecurity and fear.

The opposite of greed is generosity. A generous person by nature is focused on the needs of others instead of his own insecurity. Generosity accompanies the sincere belief that God really is taking care of the needs of His people.

Gluttony is a passion for food. It is a consequence of pride where the desire for food is so powerful that it controls life. Anything that takes over a person's ability to freely follow God is dangerous. Gluttony has been described as the callous disregard for others. A gluttonous person will stuff his face while ignoring the starving people around him. Gluttony is only a symptom of the same attitude in every area of life.

Gluttony has been linked to comfort. It is dangerous in this respect because it fosters self-reliance. Many people cope with the stress and pain in their life by eating what is popularly called "comfort food." But there is no temptation, pain or stress in anyone's life that God will not help them to sort out and take care of if they let Him.

Anger is an extreme form of pride where people react to not getting things their own way. Anger asserts a person's rights. The danger in anger, apart from the destruction it inflicts on relationships, is that it asserts privileges that are non-existent. God never promised anyone free speech or freedom to publicly worship, let alone the miniscule rights that, when denied, enflame someone's anger such as the right to not be cut off in traffic. Anger is an expression of an out of proportion need for power.

Anger is a result of a misunderstanding of authority. The antidote for anger is patience. Has God actually given us any rights beyond the right to become His child and eventually the right to the Tree of Life? He has most certainly not given us many of the rights we subconsciously claim. A key to getting rid of anger is to try to see things and understand the perspective of the one provoking the anger. Anger, like any sin, is a personal choice. An angry person is someone who chooses to be angry often enough to develop that reputation. For the one who yields to the teaching hand of God, those same trying occasions in life become the building blocks of patience.

Envy is a form of covetousness, wanting what someone else has. Envy is dangerous on two fronts. First, it may lead to stealing or adultery or even murder. More importantly, envy robs a person of God's peace and contentment. Envy ignores the fact that God made us the way we are and directs us according to a plan specifically tailored for us. It also takes the focus away from God's control in our life and places it on another person. Envy is a special form of greed that is focused on the particular possessions or accomplishments of someone else.

Envy is born out of one's discontentment with his own lot in life and it is focused on others and what they have or have achieved. Envy breeds resentment and hostility toward, most likely, an unsuspecting bystander or relation. To counter envy and its harmful consequences, one must realize that God is fully capable of providing for us and He directs us according to His plan. He is not a vending machine where everyone gets what they want and everyone gets the same thing if they just say the magic words. He leads and equips us for a special and individual purpose. When envy is held at bay, we are free to be kind toward unsuspecting bystanders or relations.

Sloth is most commonly thought of as laziness. The animal called the sloth moves so slowly that its movements are barely perceptible. Additionally, sloth has historically been defined as despondency. The danger in sloth is inaction. Certainly one of God's greatest gifts is the gift of rest; however, there is also a time for obedience and action, not action for the sake of doing something, but responding to the call of God in the day to day good works He has prepared for us to perform. Dejection and hopelessness forget the love and power of God. Sloth is the legitimate need for respite applied out of proportion. It is equivalent to sitting out the game on the sidelines dressed in full uniform, the armor of God.

The antidote for sloth is determination. The 9th chapter of John is the story of Jesus giving sight to a man who had been born blind. The chapter ties together spiritual sight and the Light of the World and juxtaposes it with spiritual blindness. Near the beginning of the chapter Jesus interjects that no one can work when the approaching darkness arrives. It is necessary to work while there is light, and there is work to be done. Like Paul implied in Galatians, there is a difference between being prepared to do battle with the adversary and actually doing battle.

The seven deadly sins form a pattern and arouse the obvious sins that flow from their motivation. No Christian is immune. A Jesuit study some years ago concluded that men most commonly struggle with lust and gluttony while women most commonly struggle with pride and envy. A wise person will take these into account when pondering forgiveness, not only taking into account that the one who wronged them struggles but that they also struggle with a fettering sin.

Forgiveness for a sin does not mean the person will never commit that sin again. God doesn't have a magic wand that he uses to tap new Christians on the head making them perfect. When the Children of Israel crossed the river Jordan into the Promised Land, they had arrived in one sense, but in another sense they had a lot of work to do. It says God rolled away their reproach when they crossed the river, but the land had to be conquered one battle at a time. Some of the land was never conquered.

Even after submitting to Jesus, Christians have arrived in one sense, but there is a lot of work that the Holy Spirit has to do in their hearts and minds. Old habits and urges must be defeated one battle at a time. Some temptations might be life-long battles. For that reason, God has not abandoned any of His children. He shares His life through His Spirit. Every Christian is born again into a body comprised of equipped and empowered believers. The important thing to remember is that every member is dealing with sin to some degree.

Forgiveness is not just a good idea, it's an

essential obligation.

"The Lord watches good people and hears their cry. The Lord forces wicked people out of His presence to blot out their memory from the earth."

Psalm – 34:15-16

ABOMINATION

The English word "abomination" comes from the Latin *abominare* which means to abhor, detest, or loathe something. These three definitions taken together come close to the meaning of abomination. "Abhor" literally means to draw back in horror. "Detest" means to pronounce or testify to the evil nature of something with the connotation of God being the witness. "Loathe" means to hate something so strongly that it hurts. When the scripture says that something is an abomination to God, it is the strongest possible way to say He hates it. God hates all sin, but not all sin is called an abomination in the scripture.

An abomination is something that is strongly hated. Yet beyond hated, abomination carries the context of the shame and disgrace associated with committing an abomination. Something abominable may also be described as vile and horrible; a revolting, repugnant object of hatred. When the scripture defines something as an abomination, it is saying that God hates it so much that it turns His stomach, in a manner of speaking.

Words and Definitions

One Greek word and several Aramaic words are translated as "abomination" by various English versions of the Bible. Sometimes, the best way to get at the meaning of a word is to look at its various synonyms. At the same time, since the words are synonyms, their definitions will be similar.

Toe'ayvah, the word most often translated "abomination", is the noun form of the verb *toe'ayv* which means to hate, loathe, abhor, or detest. *Toe'ayvah* is the thing which is hated, loathed, abhorred, or detested. It is translated as "abomination" or "abominable" most of the 126 times it occurs in the Old Testament. It is used, for example, to describe how the Egyptians felt about the Hebrews given that they were slaves and shepherds.

There are a number of things mentioned as *toe'ayvah* to God. Among those things cited, some are no surprise such as child sacrifice, idolatry, sorcery, and witchcraft. Other *toe'ayvah* practices also include impure offerings such as a prostitute's wages, the prayers of those opposed to God, corrupt scales, wickedness, pride, lying, perversion, cross dressing, and homosexuality. Notably, with the exception of dishonest scales, lying in certain circumstances and some wickedness, everything else on the list is perfectly legal and widely practiced in America. Child sacrifice is practiced with certain legal restrictions.

Shikkutz is the noun form derived from the verb *shahkats* which means to despise or regard as filthy. *Shikkutz* is the thing which is despised, filthy or abominable. The word is used 28 times in the Old Testament in 26 verses. The majority of the time, the word refers to idols, shrines built for idol worship, things sacrificed to idols, or idolatry.

Bah'ash is a root word in Aramaic which basically means to stink. No matter how it's said, to smell bad or to become odious, something's rotten. Besides being translated literally in the cases where something was really stinky as when all the fish in the Nile died from the plague of blood or when the manna was left over 'til the second day, it is also used to colorfully describe a group of people or a particular person that is hated, has an evil nature or is obnoxious. For example, the children of Israel blamed Moses for making them an abomination to Pharaoh. *Bah'ash* is only used 17 times in the Old Testament.

Shehketz is another noun derived from the verb *shahkats* which, again, means to detest or regard as filthy. Like its similar cousin, it means a detestable thing, an abhorrent thing, an idol, or an unclean thing. In almost all of the 11 times it is used in the Old Testament, it refers to the "unclean" animals which God prohibited his people from eating.

Piggool is a form of an Aramaic root word which means to stink. *Piggool* can refer to something filthy or even excrement. The four times it is used in the Old Testament, it refers to food which is prohibited from being eaten.

The only Greek word translated "abomination" is *bdeloogmah*. It is the noun form of the verb *bdeloosoe* which means to regard as vulgar, to cause to be abhorred, to turn away from due to the stench, or to detest. *Bdeloogmah* is the foul, detestable thing that is hated or turned away from. A participle form, *bdelooktoss*, is also used in the New Testament to describe something as abominable or detestable. All three forms of the word are used a total of nine times in the New Testament including the two times used to translate *shikkutz* when a passage in Daniel is referred to.

Idolatry

The Bible clearly teaches that God is love. Some people misunderstand what love is and come to the false conclusion that God cannot hate. The Bible, just as clearly, teaches that God hates sin. Some religions teach that their god is nothing more than an impersonal, positive force which is constantly and powerfully opposed to a relatively equal negative force. The God of the Bible, however, is far from being an impersonal force. The discretion, temperance, and even the forgiveness of God all derive from His personality. Love itself is a personal attribute of God.

Since God is love, anything He does flows out of His love. If God hates something, he does so because He loves man. A mother who loves her children, for example, may keep poisonous plants out of the house. If the family lives in an area where poisonous plants are abundant, she may teach her children about the dangers of the plants and instruct them to stay away from them. If one of her children died from ingesting part of a poisonous plant, it would be easy to appreciate how a hatred of the plant would develop for the sake of her other children.

In order to better understand the concept of God's hatred, an understanding of idolatry is necessary. Idolatry and the things and actions associated with it are branded an abomination to God more than anything else in the Bible.

The sin of idolatry is so critical; the first two of the Ten Commandments address it. The first addresses idolatry in a broad sense directing us to not have any gods in addition to God, not in the sense of time, but in the sense of position. In the first commandment, God makes it plain that He is to be our supreme and only God.

The second commandment addresses idolatry specifically. It prohibits the creation of any carved image in the form of any created thing for the purpose of worship or to which supernatural power is ascribed. The supernatural power could be good or evil. Examples of the types of images prohibited include Tiki dolls, Voodoo dolls, and many carved statuette idols, both of animals and manlike images, from cultures around the world and throughout history. An example of a type of image not prohibited would be the likeness of Abraham Lincoln sitting in the Lincoln Memorial to which no supernatural powers are attributed.

God prohibited idols and idolatry for many reasons. First of all, idolatry contradicts the sufficiency of God. If God is all the protection His people need, then why would they create idols to ward off evil spirits? If God is all the provision His people need, then why would they create an idol and ask it for favors? If God is always watching out for His people, then why would they create a good luck charm to help them through life?

In His wisdom, and out of His love, God prohibited idols, not because of the power in the idol, but to protect men from the fear in their hearts and their clever machinations to overcome that fear.

In one of the few times the subject is mentioned in the New Testament, Paul pointed out that idols have no real power. Depending on them for anything supernatural, good or bad, is equivalent to depending on any inanimate object for the same. No sane American today would pray to a tree for wealth or power, but cut a piece off the tree and carve a face on it and, there you have it, the tree has been cloaked with a clever and deceptive disguise.

There are, in fact, demonic spirits that take advantage of ignorant and gullible people who are easily convinced that their lucky charm works. Since God's world view includes spiritual dimensions, He also knew His prohibition of idolatry would serve to protect His people from possible demonic influence. Demonic spirits purpose to deceive men, to bring about their untimely physical death, and ultimately prolong their spiritual death or prevent them from obtaining spiritual life. The aim of demonic influence is to turn people away from God, and idolatry is one of the most effective tools at their disposal.

Idolatry is not limited to inanimate objects. God is love and the ultimate authority. The power of love goes hand in hand with the power of authority. The first commandment says in effect that nothing else and no one else loves man like God does and man is to obey nothing else and no one else who contradicts Him. Idolatry is the act of bending to the influence of something or someone in opposition to what God wants. Put simply, if a man perceives God directing him to do something, but he first checks his bank balance, his money has become an idol. If a woman knows God is leading her to do something, but she looks to see if it fits into her schedule, her agenda has become her idol. Whether they ultimately obey God or not is an important part of the issue, but the fact that they checked something else for permission reveals their heart. Idolatry in essence is the source of a person's confusion in a modern, confusing world. A heart that fully trusts God will obey Him without hesitation.

The stated reason for the second commandment is God's jealousy. Not only will God not tolerate his people flirting with other pseudo gods, He has proclaimed Himself as the ultimate avenger. The second commandment is the only commandment that pronounces a curse on its offenders. In the fourth chapter of Deuteronomy, Moses is teaching the people and warning them to refrain from idolatry after he is gone. He was certain they would grow complacent in the Promised Land. He warns them that God is an uncontrollable fire and very jealous of His people. He promises in front of heaven and earth that God will cut their lives short and completely destroy them if they stray.

The curse contained in the second commandment is very specific. The sins of the idolatrous will be inherited by their children, their grandchildren, their great-grandchildren, and their great-great-grandchildren. The commandment is phrased in the context of a hate versus love relationship. The idolatrous hate God. Those who love Him are granted clemency concerning the curse. It's interesting to note here that in the second commandment loving God is characterized by keeping His commandments. Centuries later, Jesus likewise characterized those who love Him as those who keep His commandments.

One of the key responsibilities of authority and inherent in its very nature is protection. Parents, for instance, are the primary authority of their children. They are also the primary protectors of their children. The nature of authority gives the parents the power to protect their children and their love gives them the motivation to do so.

The inherent protective ability of authority is derived from the authority's responsibility. If a boss tells a worker to do something or to do it in a particular way, the worker will not be held accountable if he does what he's told even if what he was told was wrong. The same authority that gave the boss the responsibility to give the instruction in the first place will hold him accountable for any instruction he gives. The only time this does not hold true is when the worker knows he is being told to violate a higher authority like his boss's boss.

Authority works the same way with God.

When Jesus taught His disciples to pray to God and address Him as their Father in heaven, He was conveying the parental love that God has for all His children. Just as is often true of any parent, God does not always explain why He gives certain commands. It should be enough for the children to know that God loves them and is looking out for their best interests.

The protection of God surrounds those who remain under His authority. A distraught and disillusioned father once asked a visiting pastor why God paralyzed his son from the neck down. The pastor thought it odd that God would do something like that for no reason, so he asked for the details of how the boy came to be paralyzed. It turned out that he had asked to use the family car but was denied permission by his father. He ignored his father's words and took the car without permission nonetheless. The son ignored the part of God's authority that flows through the family. After he took the car, he flew down a country back road and passed a speed limit sign that told him to slow down. He ignored the part of God's authority that flows through the government. Just prior to the intersection where the paralyzing accident occurred, the government had placed a stop sign, which the young lad also ignored. God didn't paralyze the man's son. On the contrary, out of His love for the boy, God tried at least the three times that the father could remember to prevent the accident.

The curse of the commandment against idolatry is specific. The sin of the idolater will be passed down from generation to generation. The uninformed may view it as a genetic disorder, but the curse can be broken at any time by the one who turns to God.

Let's take drinking wine for example. Drinking wine is not a sin in and of itself. But if a man is controlled by wine, then the wine becomes his idol. A man completely free from idolatry and under the authority of God is protected against all the attacks of the devil that may come against him. But if he bows down to the god of wine, a crack forms in his protection. The spiritual enemy attacks through the crack based on the idolatry to wine. The man has already been conquered by the wine and is not the focus of the attack. Instead, the enemy assaults those under the authority and protection of the man, his children. Unprotected, the children learn to bow down to their father's wine god.

The way the curse works is illustrated beautifully in the book of Job.

In the first verse of the book, Job is introduced and characterized. He is described four ways in the opening verse. First, he is called perfect, someone who is morally innocent and has strong integrity, complete and lacking nothing. Second, he is called upright or straight, someone who's on the level, correct, proper, and does the right thing. Third, he is described as someone who fears or reveres God. Last, he is described as someone who avoids evil, who makes a point to keep a safe distance from bad things, especially what he knows to be his weaknesses.

When God describes Job to Satan in the 8th

verse, using essentially the same words, He says there is no one else on the earth like him. The crux of the book of Job is the question Satan poses to God in the next couple of verses.

Before continuing in Job, it is helpful to remember that Satan, whose name means enemy, is described by Jesus as a liar and the father of lies. The question he posed to God in verses 9 and 10 is similar to the question he posed to Eve in the Garden of Eden. He used the same technique with Jesus in the wilderness. It sounded right, made sense logically, but was essentially the master con artist's hook.

Satan rhetorically asked God if the real reason Job was so righteous was because he was protected in every respect by a supernatural hedge.

The question rang true because God had indeed placed a hedge of protection around Job, his possessions and his work and its results. Job was not a victim of the curse revealed in the second commandment. Idolatry was the farthest thing from his heart and he, therefore, reaped the benefits in his life. As God allowed the pieces of the hedge to come down, Job continued to demonstrate his integrity, his reverence for God, and that he truly was unique among men.

By the end of the book, Job confessed his faith in God, and God restored the hedge of protection around him. God demonstrated to Satan through Job that the protection was the result of righteousness, not the cause of it.

Idolatry sends the message to God that He is incapable or cannot be trusted. It begins subtly and grows like a cancer. It is no wonder why

God hates it.

Homosexuality

Homosexuality is mentioned here because it is directly called an abomination five times in the Bible and indirectly many more. The topic will be discussed in depth in a later chapter.

"The two were naked,
Adam and his wife,
and it was not
shameful."

Genesis – 2:25

SEX

Why Sex

After serving only a few months as a prison chaplain, a young minister stopped asking the inmates why they were in the pen. That's because he always got the same answer. With few exceptions, the younger ones had been convicted of some sort of drug violation while most of the older ones were serving time for a sex crime.

Americans seem to have more sex hang-ups than people in any other country in the world. The sad reality is that the church in America, instead of standing apart, is just as immersed in America's moral problems as those outside her doors. Instead of having some impact on society, the church today finds itself constantly trying to catch up to its own standards. Some estimates run as high as one in six evangelical pastors having serious problems with sexual relationships. All too frequently, high profile pastors and evangelists are in the news for adulterous relationships or sex related problems. Too many times, priests have made the news for sexually victimizing children.

Evangelization of a dying nation becomes all the more difficult when the power of God makes no difference in the attitudes and behavior of those He supposedly recreated and sanctified.

With all the problems caused by sex, one might ask why God would create sex at all.

It's interesting to note that the creation of man is first mentioned in the 27th verse of the Bible. The very next verse recounts that God blessed the man and gave him his first command. Long before the Ten Commandments and prior to the instructions in the Garden of Eden, God told the man, "Be fruitful and multiply." In other words, the first thing the Bible records God telling man to do is to have sex.

The first and most obvious reason for sex is that of procreation. Literally, the command was to fill the earth; a task that would take many centuries and countless generations. If God was serious about filling the earth, the sex drive would have to be strong enough to make it a priority in the man's psyche.

Having already discussed God's loving nature, it follows that something as important as sex would also be pleasurable for man. Obeying God's command to have sex fulfills His wish to populate the earth and also rewards the man as he obeys. According to the book of Hebrews, believing that God rewards those who follow Him is an essential aspect of the faith that pleases Him. Sex is the first example of that principle in action.

Let me interject a reminder about the definition of sin as missing the mark. God created sex as a good thing. When used properly there are incalculable rewards. But as demonstrated in the Garden of Eden, the devil twists and perverts just enough to distract, confuse and defeat mankind. Even well intentioned Christians can become the devil's advocate when they try to redefine what the scripture teaches.

One of the most damaging misconceptions Christians have about sex is that it is a necessary evil for procreation that should be stoically avoided at all other costs. Perhaps that idea derived from the mistaken perception that David was talking about his parents having sex when he said he was conceived in sin. Psalm 51, written after his adultery with Bathsheba, is a plea for forgiveness wherein David is expressing his total sinfulness from conception to death. He confesses his utter unworthiness for the forgiveness he is pleading to receive and throws himself on the mercy of God's court. To further clarify David's assertion, the first part of Ezekiel 18 explains that God does not hold children accountable for the sins of their parents.

The language used in the Song of Solomon describes sex as a delightful activity. Again, Paul revealed that he understood the need and enjoyment of sex when he gave instructions to married couples to refrain from depriving each other of sex unless by agreement for a fixed time.

In yet another instruction, Hebrews 13 teaches that sex within marriage is pure and unstained, morally speaking.

So, sex is the vehicle God created for procreation. Just as He made food tasty and nature awesome to behold, He made sex fun and rewarding.

Joining in Unity

On several occasions during Jesus' ministry, the Sadducees or Pharisees would try to involve Him in their own debate about theological issues and their squabbling over differences in scripture interpretation. They were trying to get Him to choose a side and validate their own arguments. On one such occasion, recorded both in the gospels of Matthew and Mark, the Pharisees asked Jesus for His opinion on divorce. They asked Him, in essence, what He thought were legitimate grounds for a divorce.

Here as on other occasions, He marveled at their ignorance of the scriptures. He asked them if they were familiar with the fact that God created man male and female from the beginning. He told them that marriage was based on that act of creation. When God created Eve, Adam's reaction was, "This is me!" Marriage is the rejoining of Adam, male and female. It's important to note here that Eve was not a duplicate of Adam but a complement to Adam.

On a related note, the Pharisees asked Jesus why God permitted the people to divorce their wives in the first place. To understand Jesus' answer we must look at the circumstances surrounding God's decision.

The scene was the Sinai wasteland. The time was after the ten spies had returned from the land of promise. The people grumbled and complained to Moses about a man having to stay married when he was unhappy with his wife. They asked him for permission to divorce, and God granted it. Who were these people? They were the same ones who sided with the spies that doubted God. They were the people that wanted to return to slavery in Egypt; the same ones that God had already threatened to destroy and would have been dead had Moses not intervened on their behalf. These were the people that God swore would never see the land. They had tried God's patience over and over again. They were already doomed, wandering the desert, waiting to die so that God could bring their children into the land. These were the people that asked for permission to divorce their wives. Jesus said that God acquiesced due to the stubbornness of their hearts.

When Jesus answered the Sadducees and Pharisees, He gave further admonition that people shouldn't undo what God has done, specifically, joining of the husband and wife in heaven. In one of the most repeated verses in scripture He declares that the man and his wife will become one flesh. That is not to say united physically, though it is through physical union that the marriage is made complete. The word translated "flesh" in Genesis 2:24 is a noun which can also mean skin or meat. That is to say, they will be one body just as the church is the body of Christ. Jesus further implies that they are made one spirit by revealing that God joins husband and wife in heaven.

Adultery

Most everyone understands that adultery is the act of sex involving someone who is married and someone who is not their spouse. Not everyone understands why the term adultery is used.

"Adultery" is a particular noun form (the act) of the verb, "adulterate", (the action). Both derive from the Latin *adulterare* which means to falsify or corrupt. The term adulterate means to take something pure and make it impure by adding something else; deception and inferior quality or value is implied.

Before authorities were wary, adulteration would show up every once in a while in the newspaper when, for example, the owner of a gasoline station would add water or some other cheap liquid into his storage tanks to stretch the value of the gas. The headline would read, "So and So Station Caught Selling 'Adulterated' Gas." For the same reason today, gasoline which has been diluted with ethanol or some other additive must clearly be labeled as such.

Adulteration is a deceptive method of passing off something cheap for more than it's worth. Again, for example, grape juice is considerably cheaper than wine. A host at a large party can provide five gallons of wine for a little more than the cost of four by mixing in one gallon of grape juice with the four gallons of wine. With the intention of deceiving the guests, the host has adulterated the pure wine by diluting it with the cheaper grape juice. If the host informs the guests that the wine has been sweetened with grape juice then the term adulteration doesn't apply since the guests realize they are drinking a mixed drink and not pure wine.

The term adultery is applied to sex outside a marriage because the same principles apply.

When a marriage is consummated, a new entity is born which is the marriage itself. Man and wife are joined spiritually at that point. Evidence of that fact is found in 1st Corinthians chapter six in the last half dozen verses. There, Paul begins a short warning by reminding the Corinthians that they are spiritually one with Christ and members of His Body. He quotes the same passage from Genesis 2 that Jesus quoted to the Pharisees, telling the Corinthians that having sex with a prostitute results in the same kind of joining that happens in marriage and also joins the Body of Christ to the prostitute. Since we know that Paul wrote the letter to Corinth after the crucifixion and resurrection of Jesus, it follows that the union that takes place during sex must also be a spiritual union.

The marriage that is born takes on a life of its own and grows and matures over time. A new marriage has the same level of maturity as a newborn baby which can only sleep, cry, and make a mess in its diaper on its own. A newborn marriage needs the love and nurturing of caring elders just as much as a newborn baby needs help to eat, burp, dress, and clean up the mess in its diaper.

As the marriage grows, it remains pure as long as the man and wife remain faithful to each other sexually. If one of the two has sex with someone outside of their marriage, it's called adultery for good reasons.

First of all, deception is undoubtedly involved. The unfaithful partner tries to go on as if nothing has happened, continuing to defraud his/her spouse. This ordinarily doesn't succeed because of the nature of the spiritual union between husband and wife. Our five senses let us know the condition of the physical world surrounding us. In the same way, our spiritual senses inform us of the spiritual environment we find ourselves in. In particular, the condition of the partner with whom we are bound together spiritually. Spiritual intuition is a type of extra sensory perception; the partner knows something has happened as surely as if they were in the room while it was going on. They can't explain why they know, they just know that they know.

Second, an adulterous relationship is of inferior or cheapened quality. Sex is not marriage and marriage is not sex. Sex apart from marriage is nothing more than basic animal instinct gratification. Sex is not the basis of marital love, respect, support or security. So, sex outside of marriage is, basically, at least one person using and defrauding the other for their own selfish gratification. That is one of the reasons that adulterous relationships tend not to work out when the adulterer divorces his or her spouse for the object of the affair.

Lastly, and most importantly, adultery adulterates the marriage. In the same way the Corinthians were joining the Body of Christ to prostitutes, an adulterer joins the body of his/her spouse to the lover. Adultery does not break the spiritual bond between husband and wife; it brings an additional spirit into the relationship. That is why the offended spouse knows. The marriage which was once a pure relationship is now polluted by the addition of a foreign spirit, one not a part of the covenant of the marriage.

Many Christians erroneously believe that adultery means the end of the marriage. If that were the case, it would not be called adultery but something more along the lines of "murdery" or perhaps "suicidery." It is most certainly not a scriptural justification for divorce.

Jesus spoke of divorce twice in Matthew, first in chapter five and then again in chapter nineteen. A careful reading of the two verses further illustrates adultery. In 5:32 Jesus said that whoever divorces his wife forces her to commit adultery and whoever marries a divorced woman commits adultery. In 19:9 He says that whoever divorces his wife and marries another woman commits adultery and whoever marries a divorced woman commits adultery. The only exception in both cases is if illicit sex, or adultery, has already occurred. In all cases, the adultery refers to the contamination of the original marriage.

In order to adulterate something, it must be pure. Adulteration is a true/false state, once true it remains true. Once something has been adulterated it is no longer pure and can therefore not be adulterated again. Things are usually adulterated for profit. Illicit drugs are often adulterated by unscrupulous suppliers in order to increase the quantity and get more money for the same amount of pure drug. The additives used to cut the drug can sometimes be more harmful than the drug itself. Corrupt meat suppliers may inject water into chicken or salt water into pork to increase the weight and thereby the cost of the meat. In each case, once the product is adulterated, it cannot be adulterated again since it is no longer pure. After the water is dirty, it doesn't make any difference how dirty.

When a marriage has been adulterated or made spiritually impure, divorce and remarriage don't change that condition. So in the case of a man whose wife has committed adultery, if he divorces her he can't do any more damage to his marriage in terms of spiritual purity than has already been done. If she remarries, she will not adulterate her marriage because it is no longer pure.

On the other hand, Jesus makes it clear that the act of divorce does not dissolve the marriage. Otherwise, remarriage would not result in the adultery of a marriage where both partners had remained faithful to each other. Adultery only has meaning in the context of such a marriage.

There is no action that man can take to separate that spiritual union. Scripture does teach that death breaks the union thus allowing widows and widowers to remarry freely without condemnation. In fact, the Old Testament goes so far as to specify who is in line to marry a widow in order that she is protected and cared for.

In the opening verses of Romans chapter seven, Paul sheds a little more light on the act of adultery. The spiritual laws in place for our existence here are in effect as long as we live just as the law of gravity affects us as long as we have a physical body on this planet. When either the husband or the wife dies, their spirit moves on, and the remaining partner is no longer joined to them. Hence, there is no spiritual union to adulterate.

The Whole Land Polluted

The fact that the divorce of a faithful couple would lead to adultery down the road teaches that the spiritual union of the original marriage remains intact until one of the couple dies. The state of that spiritual union may vary from pure to totally polluted, but man does not have the power or authority to separate what God has joined.

The Bible talks directly about divorce in fewer than a dozen passages. In several passages, the reality of the spiritual bond of marriage is illustrated. In the opening verses of Deuteronomy 24, the law states that a man must not remarry his divorced wife if she has married someone else in the interim. Jeremiah 3 refers to that law and explains that in the event this practice is widespread in Israel, then the land would become totally polluted. Just as adultery destroys the purity of a marriage, serial adultery on a wide scale destroys the purity of the nation. The principle is as true for America today as it was when Jeremiah was warning Judah just prior to their being taken away into exile by the Babylonians.

It's normal to see one's own faults as minor

while sitting in judgment of others. It often takes a third party to point out the plank in the eye of the judge. Purity should start within the house and people of God. Remember that the people who threw the adulteress at Jesus' feet were self-proclaimed pious leaders of the community. We would likewise do well to remember John Bradford's words when he looked out from his cell in the Tower of London and saw a group being led to their execution: "There, but for the grace of God, goes John Bradford."

As the nation continues to ignore the warnings in scripture, even men of faith pay the price in their own spirits and continue to masquerade as though nothing has happened. The warnings are clear. Ecclesiastes 5:5-6; failure to hold to vows made to God results in His anger and the work of one's hands being destroyed. Malachi 2:13-14; God refuses offerings because He has witnessed the treachery of the priest with his wife. 1st Peter 3:7; men, love and honor your wife or God will stop listening to your prayers.

In 1st Thessalonians 4, Paul emphasizes that God wants his people to avoid adultery. He says that Christians should not be controlled by their passions like those people who do not know God.

With divorce and adultery so prevalent among God's people in America, even among the clergy, is it any wonder why churches are declining, God's blessings are waning and prayers go unanswered? God has not changed the way He deals with man. Just as Job's blessings and protection were the result of his righteousness and not the cause, the rampant unrighteousness in America is the cause of a loss of spiritual protection and blessing.

But there is always hope with God. For as many warnings as there are, there are also promises. In 2nd Chronicles 7:14, He promises to heal the land if His people turn to Him and away from their wickedness. Again in the first chapter of Isaiah; make yourself clean, turn from evil, and He will make the bloodiest sins as white as snow. Jesus, who was the embodiment of God's hope, said on several occasions that anything is possible with God. Even in the Garden of Gethsemane He said that it was possible for the crucifixion to be avoided if God wanted it that way.

It requires a tremendous swallowing of pride to admit sin. As a rule, people are uncomfortable admitting their mistakes, and they try instead to justify everything they do. But the only way for us to move forward into purity is to admit our shortcomings to God and, when applicable, to those we have wronged. Humility before God puts a man back on proper footing and restores God's blessings.

Adultery is not the unforgivable sin. When John said in the first chapter of his first letter that God will totally wash us from the effects of any sin we confess, that included the spiritual pollution of adultery and all the side effects.

The key to purity is a heart that seeks God above anything else. We do not have the power to bring about our own purity, but God does. God's promises are fulfilled to those who are willing to admit their guilt and seek forgiveness.

Marriage

It's interesting to note that in many languages, in addition to Greek and Aramaic, the word for woman is the same as the word for wife.

The concept of marriage is well defined in the Old Testament even though there is not a lot of specific instruction. Malachi teaches that marriage is a covenant. Most of the instructional references to marriage in the Bible are found in the New Testament.

In Ephesians 5, Paul gives instructions to the husband and wife about their relationship to each other. At the end of the instruction he says he is also talking about the relationship between Christ and the church.

The message to the wife is simple. Submit to the husband as you would to the Lord. Paul is not asking the wife to do anything that the church should not be doing in its relationship to Christ. And in submitting, she is likely to meet her husband's deepest emotional need, that of self-respect. The example for her to follow is Jesus, who submitted His will to the Father, knowing it would mean a painful death.

Submission of one's will is not a demeaning act and does not imply any lesser value or ability. Jesus is equal with God in every respect but authority. And even though God delegated all His authority to His son, Jesus is seated at the Father's right hand, still subject to His authority. Paul does not teach anywhere that the husband is in any way better than the wife. The husband has been tasked with the responsibility of delegating God's authority in his marriage.

The message to the husband is also simple. Love your wife with the same self-sacrificing attitude that Jesus had for the church. Paul is basically asking the husband to put himself in Jesus' place as the benefactor of the church. By following Christ's example he is likely to meet his wife's deepest emotional need of security. The example is spelled out in the instruction. Jesus laid down His life for the good of the church with the goal of purifying and setting the church apart for Himself. The husband is to follow Jesus' example and lay down his life out of love for his wife.

Peter puts the message to the husband in slightly different terms. 1st Peter 3:7 is one of the most mistranslated and also misunderstood verses in the Bible. First, Peter implies that a husband already knows how to live with his wife and that he should live with her accordingly. He gives the example of a weaker vessel (Greek – *asthenestero skeuei*).

Even today, in our homes we have dishes (vessels) that are fragile and dishes that are nearly indestructible. Thick plastic or rubber cups, bowls, and plates can be safely put into the hands of children and tossed haphazardly into the sink. Technology has given us very nice looking dishes that can be handled roughly and without care. They might be referred to as everyday dishes.

The more fragile vessels are made of materials like porcelain, crystal, or china. They require more care, even during the manufacturing process, and are therefore more costly. People who own them know at the time of purchase how fragile they are. Such dishes are neither handled roughly, nor entrusted to the hands of young children. They are gently placed in the sink and washed tenderly. They are also usually stored in a glass front cabinet where they are proudly displayed.

Peter instructs the husband to treat his wife with similar care. Treat her with the same respect and tenderness that you would treat your china, porcelain, or crystal. He does not even imply that she is, in fact, weaker or fragile. She may be stronger in many ways which, nevertheless, does not invalidate Peter's instruction to appreciate her as rare, delicate, and valuable.

Both husband and wife can look to Jesus as their example. He showed us how to love and how to obey.

A marriage that follows the will of God is a living testimony to the nature of God. While it is true that the testimony may be received by strangers, the most important recipients are the children within the family. Even with little specific instruction, a child raised in a home where the marriage follows God's principles will learn of the nature and love of God intuitively. They will also learn to trust God.

A marriage which is nothing more than a selfish contract with both partners getting what they can out of it will produce children that don't trust God. Children raised in homes without God grow up confused and self-seeking, living their lives as they subconsciously learned from their parents. Their marriages are likely to be disasters because they know nothing of what real love is about and instead struggle with their own insecurities.

The biblical model of marriage is not a contract where each partner is responsible for his or her share, fifty/fifty, in a manner of speaking. Instead, it is a mutual solemn agreement on the part of both to be 100 percent committed to their respective responsibilities. Peter goes so far as to say that if even one of the partners is faithful to God's principles, it is enough to restore the marriage.

Sex is not the basis of marriage. Sex is instead one of the rewarding responsibilities of marriage. It is the icing on the cake. In addition to the means of having children, sex provides the timely gentle nudges to make a good marriage better. Sex alone, however, cannot save a bad marriage.

The Holy Spirit specifically predicted that as time goes on, some will abandon the faith as they pay attention to confusing spirits and the teaching of demons. They impart the hypocritical lies they learn since their conscience is dead.

- Paul – 1Timothy 4:1, 2

PERVERSION

Two Aramaic words are translated as "perverted" in the Old Testament. One means to stretch out, as one might say the serpent stretched the truth when it spoke to Eve in the Garden of Eden. The other means to bend or twist something.

The word, "perversion" is sometimes applied to specific actions, but the basic meaning of the principle is the same. When something is perverted, it is distorted, such as a perverted outcome which is an unexpected deviation from the intended course. Perversion can also refer to something that is unnatural or corrupt. In that sense, it only has meaning in reference to something pure.

Even the purest of motives and intentions can result in perverse consequences. For example, decades ago when a city in Vietnam tried to eradicate a harmful rat population, the government came up with an ingenious plan. They offered to pay for every rat tail turned in by the people. Instead of eradicating the rats, however, the people started breeding them.

Perversion is inescapably common today. In the media, the polite term for perversion is spin. There are even professional "Spin Doctors" who make their living twisting the words or perceptions of others to make them conform to what their employers want to be said. Again, how often is the story reported by a press organization exactly opposite from what the headline infers?

Perversion is a subtle form of dishonesty, capable of ensnaring the unwary. It is also the set of circumstances and lifestyle the unsuspecting find themselves in when they believe and follow lies that twist the truths of God.

The Unpardonable Sin

The most severe form of perversion can lead to the unpardonable sin.

There are two places in scripture that talk about the unpardonable sin; the first is in the book of Deuteronomy. Toward the end of the book, Moses is giving the nation of Israel final instructions before they cross the river Jordan into the land they were promised. Chapter 28 includes a long list of blessings that will follow the people if they trust God and obey. Conversely, the chapter also states that disobedience will bring about a long list of curses instead of blessing.

Moses begins chapter 29 by reminding the people of all they had seen in their wandering, both good and bad. He reminded them of the hard times, the times God performed fantastic miracles for them, the battles they had already won, and the supernatural way God had taken care of them. He also reminded them of the man-made idols that they saw and how the people they encountered worshipped them.

Here, in the infant stages of the nation which God chose to be His people, He showed them the difference between a living, caring, powerful God, and the lifeless, cold renditions of man's imagination and superstitions.

With that introduction, Moses gave the nation a severe warning, one of the most serious in the Old Testament. The warning was directed at the man who was thinking about turning away from God to the false gods of his neighbors. The grave sin was not simply turning away, but being comfortable in the delusion that he could do whatever his heart desired and get away with it, essentially declaring through his actions that God does not punish the wicked and reward the righteous.

Moses warned that such a man would be singled out by God for special punishment and he would never be forgiven.

The more familiar expression of the unpardonable sin is found in the New Testament in Matthew 12 and Mark 3. Matthew is referred to most often, probably because his gospel records what may have been the precipitating event that motivated Jesus to talk about it.

On that particular occasion when a possessed man who was also blind and mute was brought to Jesus, He healed him. This prompted the Pharisees to remark that the only power Jesus was using to exorcise demons was the power of the devil. Jesus pointed out the fallacy in their logic, and then gave them a strict warning. He told them that blasphemy of the Spirit of God is the only sin that God will not forgive.

Blasphemy of the Spirit is the result of a perverted mind. It is not a condition that man is born with but the end of a process that begins in the heart. Jeremiah cautions that man's heart is beyond understanding in its cunning and mischief. It wants what it wants and will find a way to get it, rationalizing and justifying any means.

Blasphemy of the Spirit is considering the good work of the Holy Spirit evil or praising evil as though it was the work of the Holy Spirit. It is a state of perversion someone reaches when he redefines God for himself in his own interest, seeing what is in reality good as bad and what is in reality bad as good. The saddest part about someone in such deceptive circumstances is that he does not know he is deceived.

Jesus warned the Pharisees when they ascribed the good work He was doing to the power of the devil. They probably believed what they were saying due to the self-interests of their hearts. They couldn't fit Jesus into their theological framework so they concluded that, since He was just an ordinary sinner, He could not possibly have such power. They may have also reasoned that, since He was not of any religious order, His power came straight from the devil. The pride concerning the status and position they held and their natural self-doubt probably contributed to their perspective. They had it all figured out and truly believed that they were doing the right thing before God.

The Deceived vs. the Wicked

In the middle ages, the church was desperately short of the funds needed to build the basilica in Rome. It went to great lengths to raise cash from every corner of the empire. Offerings were scant as the majority of the church was poor, and a significant part of the economy at the time was based on the exchange of goods and services instead of money. One way the church motivated the people to give money was to teach that their offerings would guarantee their deceased relatives entrance into heaven. It also sold permission to sin.

These teachings were untrue, but the people didn't know it. They could not read, for the most part, and certainly couldn't read the scripture since it was only available in Latin. They went along with what they were taught, believing their teachers. The people were deceived.

Presently, preachers and teachers of doctrine abound. Not all of them have pure motives. Not all of them make the effort to diligently study the scripture. Many voices blare out without having any depth or personal understanding of their own whatsoever and simply repeat what they heard someone else say.

The majority of Americans inherited their faith from their parents. They believe what they think their parents believed and have no idea why their parents believed it. They just assume it's in the Bible somewhere. They are deceived.

To be deceived can be compared to walking barefoot in a dark room while trying to negotiate the obstacles and avoid the walls. The darkness doesn't make the obstacles disappear. Any obstacle in the chosen path will be discovered in due course and may cause an injury. In the darkness, the walls will probably be found before the door is, unless the walker already knows the way because he has seen the room in the light.

No one deceives himself intentionally. The deceived believe and trust a lie they heard from someone else. If the person they decided to trust is deceived, the deception only multiplies. The most important thing to understand about those who are deceived is that they do not know they are deceived. They are sincere in their beliefs, however misguided.

There are countless false doctrines being taught that masquerade as Christian. Well thought out, intricate, and highly refined, they mislead many innocent followers away from the truths of scripture. The deception is subtle, like the question the serpent posed to Eve in the Garden of Eden or the suggestions the devil gave to Jesus in the wilderness before He began His ministry. These doctrines should be suspect if they rely on bizarre interpretations of scripture. Doctrines are equally suspicious when they read into a passage of scripture something which is not stated. But regrettably, people tend to believe people they like or find attractive and they let the bizarre slip by.

False and confusing doctrines are not new. In the New Testament, Paul constantly preached against false doctrines. Some were the result of misunderstanding, but others were deliberately spread by fanatical individuals with an agenda to discredit Jesus' teaching and confuse new believers. Paul understood their motives and perspective because he too had been deceived.

How can a Christian test a doctrine to avoid being deceived? In the seventh chapter of the gospel of Matthew, Jesus gives us the answer. The result of the principle when taken to extreme will reveal if it is from God or Satan. If the end result is spiritual life for everyone involved, the teaching is from God. If the end result is the temporal benefit of an individual or a group of individuals and the exclusion of others, the teaching is from the deceiver. Is the teacher a shepherd or a wolf?

Only the most naïve would have difficulty in believing that there are wicked people roaming this earth. There truly are individuals who get satisfaction and enjoyment out of causing others to suffer. More than merely words to an old Johnny Cash song, there are people who have indeed killed someone just for the thrill of watching them die. There are people so callous that they are incapable of feeling or empathy.

Unlike the deceived, the wicked know what they are doing. They feed on the rush of rebellion. It's not enough for them to go their own way; they justify and push their corruption to gain a following. The bigger their following, the more justified they feel.

The restriction against eating pork can be used to illustrate the difference between the deceived and the wicked. Suppose a person hears from one extra-biblical source or another that it is a sin to eat pork. Trusting the source to be true, they in turn teach others that eating pork is a sin. So far, the person is deceived, honestly and sincerely believing his teaching to be correct. Along the way he is shown the many passages in the New Testament that show that eating pork is no longer a sin. If he continues to teach to the contrary, he has crossed the line from deceived to wicked. In other words, he teaches in opposition to what he knows the New Testament to say.

The biggest motivator of deception is our own heart. Jeremiah pointed out that our own hearts trick us by deception. Accordingly, both the Old and New Testaments teach that God judges men according to their hearts. Words and actions are only the fruit of the heart's pursuits. It is on that account that deception is difficult to catch. Everyone believes their heart is right, and consequently, hearts are slow to change.

One might expect churches to be the least vulnerable to deception, but they are made up of people with hearts. A church becomes exposed to deception when it strays in its mission from Jesus' stated purposes of first, seeking and saving the lost and second, feeding and equipping the sheep. A church becomes exposed to deception when it takes direction from something besides the Bible and abandons prayer, fellowship, and the ministry of the Word of God.

Churches fall into a serious pitfall when they take their eyes off Jesus and focus on themselves. All too often churches become business enterprises or social clubs weighted down with legalism designed to extol their own virtues and keep out the undesirables. In the name of setting an example, they shun or cast out the very people that should be at the focus of their mission. They confuse mission work with a foreign land and forget that the mission is inside, outside, and all around their building.

It's easy to point a condemning finger at the self-professed atheist and forget that all men will stand before God and give an account of their actions and attitudes, the sinner and the Pharisee. Jesus told a parable about a sinner and a Pharisee who each prayed to God. The sinner's prayer was a simple, penitent plea for mercy; the Pharisee's prayer was a prideful boast. The Pharisee was deceived.

A Gift from the Enemy

On a journey to the moon, if the course is miscalculated by the tiniest fraction of a degree, the moon will be missed by hundreds of miles unless course corrections are made along the way. On the journey of life, even the smallest perversion can send us off into darkness, confusion, sin, and pain unless repentance and correction are made along the way.

In the New Testament, Satan, an Aramaic name which means "enemy" or "accuser", is often called the devil, a Greek term which means "deceiver". Our spiritual adversary, the deceiver, barely needs to prompt our own hearts to head us in a direction away from God because all men are born selfish. Call it by whatever fancy name or instinct, man's selfish nature is evident from early childhood. Man naturally doesn't want God. He doesn't want anyone telling him what to do; instead, he wants to be his own god.

Satan is only too happy to help man get his wish. So, in the garden, he told Eve that she could be just like God if she ate the forbidden fruit. Satan also played on Jesus' humanity when he told Him that He could have everything in the world if He would only bow down and worship him. His tactics haven't changed in thousands of years, probably because they work so well on an ever gullible mankind. Eat the forbidden fruit, and you can be just like God, able to decide what's right and wrong for you. Follow the devil, and you can get ahead in life, a shortcut to everything you ever wanted.

Perversion is difficult to detect because it sounds right and looks good. One example of devastation wrought by perversion can be seen in a particular teaching of the white supremacist movement. One of their popular doctrines says that they are the chosen race of God. They believe this based on the doctrine of Anglo-Israelism, an idea that surfaced in Britain back in the 17th century.

According to the false doctrine, the Ten Lost Tribes of Israel moved to Europe and eventually found their way to the British Isles. The white supremacists pick verses of what they call prophecy from all over the Old Testament to prove the doctrine is true. Their so called proof is very compelling to those who know little or nothing of biblical history, such as the members of the militias they recruit in prisons across America. The doctrine looks and sounds right and, by virtue of its biblical source, engenders fervent passion for their cause.

The teaching was originally touted to enhance

the pride of the British people and prove the divine right of rule of the British monarch who was also deceptively alleged to be a direct descendant of David, the second king of Israel. In modern times it has evolved to become a rationale for racist hatred by those who are deceived by it.

After the death of Solomon, Israel split into two kingdoms. Ten tribes formed a kingdom in the north and the remaining 2 tribes formed the southern realm. At that time, Assyria was the dominant power and taxed the northern kingdom heavily. After over a decade of trouble from the tiny kingdom, Assyria conquered the territory and took most of its inhabitants away. But unlike the Babylonians, Assyria had a different philosophy of dealing with seized troublesome nations. They broke up families and disbursed the people throughout their empire thus permanently destroying any nationalistic hope of restoration. The northern tribes were indeed lost, not in the sense that they were intact someplace nobody could find, but that they no longer existed. Even if they were intact, no descendant of David ever ruled in the northern kingdom of Israel. David was from the tribe of Judah whose descendants are among us today.

Anglo-Israelism has been disproven by archeologists, linguists, and geneticists, but the perversion continues to be believed.

Further damage is done because there are those outside the church who know nothing of the true God and hear someone espousing the biblical justification for racial bigotry. Consequently, they brush off the legitimacy of

the Bible completely and may consider all
Christians to be small minded followers of
outdated superstitions and unfounded fears. In
so doing and to the devil's delight, they alienate
themselves from the truth.

So the little lie motivated by Satan way back
in the 17th century to bolster the pride and
legitimacy of the king's rule has come full circle
and borne the fruit of its maker. A key to
understanding here is that the Bible legitimizes
government authority without the need to resort
to any perversion. But using a legitimate
sounding hook, Satan sneaked in the
acceptability of pride. Just as he slipped in the
valid need to eat in the temptation to eat the
forbidden fruit. A partial lie is still a lie.

In 2nd Corinthians 11, Paul reprimanded the
Corinthians for the ease with which they
accepted every deluded and lying preacher who
came their way. False teachers are nothing new.
Jesus warned about them at the conclusion of the
Sermon on the Mount calling them wolves in
sheep's clothing. Paul warns that they appear to
be apostles of Christ, which shouldn't surprise
anyone since Satan changes himself into an
angel of light. Legitimate looking and sounding
teachers who teach half-truths generate serious
damage in the church with far reaching
consequences.

If the true ministers and the deceivers look
alike, what hope is there for those looking to do
the right thing? Jesus said that the
consequences of their actions and teachings will
expose the imposter. Paul gives a pretty good
account of what to look for, both good and bad, in

Galatians chapter five. The surest way to protect oneself from false teaching is to read and memorize the scripture. Know it inside and out. Know it in context.

In his first letter, John sums up the human motivations of perversion as everything in the world, specifically, whatever people are tempted to experience, whatever people are tempted to see, and whatever people want others to think of them. The experience could also include meeting a legitimate need in an illegitimate way.

Satan uses the circumstances in which we find ourselves in combination with those three motivations. In the garden, Satan told Eve, "You will be like God." The fruit was already there on the tree. Eve was motivated to disobey God when she imagined it was good food, when she rationalized that it was pretty fruit, and when she believed that she would be important. Regrettably, the serpent's lie suppressed the truth that Eve was already like God. She had been created in His image. She was already important to Him.

While it was the act of disobedience which was the sin, a pattern of thoughts and beliefs always precede the action. Jesus went so far as to say that the thoughts of sinful action that precede the acts are just as culpable in the eyes of God.

It's interesting to note that the same God who destroyed the earth with a flood in the days of Noah, who told Moses to separate himself from the people so He could destroy the children of Israel and start over, spared the lives of Adam and Eve.

The Slippery Slope to Perversion

The apostle Paul gives a quick summary of the road to perversion in the first chapter of his letter to the Romans. The transition to perversion happens on both an individual, personal level and on a national, imperial level. On an individual level, the process can take years while on a national level it can take decades, or even centuries.

The guiding hand in the transition to perversion is that of the devil. The incremental, barely perceptible steps along the way are clearly seen in hindsight, but difficult to detect or guard against while they are happening. For that reason it's important to hear the voice of God and be sensitive to the promptings of the Spirit along the way. That is not to say that the devil forces anyone to do anything. If that were the case, no one would be responsible for his own sin. He merely incites temptation with a constant shower of lies.

The process begins with pride; when men are proud of their own wisdom and understanding; when men think they have it all figured out, God ceases to be a necessity for them and so ceases to be relevant. Present day arguments by atheists against the existence of God center on their perceived lack of His necessity. They reason that since it wasn't necessary for God to be involved in the creation of the world, He wasn't. They believe that things just happened by themselves according to the natural laws that man has figured out. Individually, they choose to avoid God because they think they are getting along fine without Him.

When a person takes his eyes off of God, who is the source of truth and knowledge, he begins the journey toward perversion. The same principle applies on a national level, that is, a nation begins its journey toward perversion by turning away from God. In ancient times, men created idols to use as a replacement for God. Today, men are bold enough to claim to be their own god. In either case the result is the same. Man goes after materialistic rewards and sets his self-centered affections on things and people.

In the course of transition to perversion, God's intentions and leadership become unimportant. Man is convinced of his own superior intellect and devises intricate methods to satisfy every want. Solomon, out of his own curiosity, studied man's pursuits and came to the conclusion that all of them are hollow and pointless. He talks about his findings in the book of Ecclesiastes.

Without the influence of God, men gradually develop an appetite for the revolting. When their self-centered cravings control them, they no longer care about others and become callous and abusive. Eventually their relationships begin to fall apart as they become suspicious and treacherous toward others. The further they move away from God, the more they take on the personality of a merciless sociopath, often hiding behind a big smile and social pleasantries.

The final step into perversion is the approval and encouragement of others who are similarly engaged.

Nations began the slide toward perversion in earnest beginning with a period now referred to as the "Age of Enlightenment." Satan's motivational pitch was almost identical to his encouraging Eve to eat the forbidden fruit: "Your eyes will be opened." Men who proclaimed their own wisdom and superiority relied on science to attempt to disprove the teachings of the church, and gullible, ignorant Christians were all too quick to believe them.

Science is not the enemy; however, one must be careful with science for several reasons. Science is merely the process of guessing how something works, setting up the conditions to test the guess, and seeing if it really works as guessed. Science is moved along by the documentation of the results. The scientific method can be tricky, though, because all of the variables involved in the guess may not be known, depending on the scale of the guess. To get dependable results, variables must be able to be controlled to make it possible to isolate what is being proven.

So-called scientific results can be misleading when the one doing the testing is more interested in proving the guess than discovering the truth. This can happen when variables are purposefully manipulated or when results to the contrary are purposefully hidden or discounted. Frequently, scientists have to fill in the blanks when something can't be seen, certain variables cannot be controlled, or the variables cannot be duplicated. They also must interpolate results when the instruments used to measure the results are not accurate enough to adequately prove or disprove the guess.

Results attributed to science can also be flat

out wrong when the one doing the test sees what he wants to see instead of what is there. That is not necessarily due to any malicious intent of the observer. The human brain itself plays tricks on us. We are not aware of the blind spot in each of our eyes because our brain fills in the gap with what is not really there. Optical illusions work because our brain actively and subconsciously is involved in translating the information sent by our eyes. The Gestalt principles work because the human brain naturally creates wholes out of pieces, filling in the blanks. Proofreading is difficult because our brains automatically correct spelling mistakes.

Responsible science is a gift from God. The fruits of responsible science include technology and all manner of improvements on the human condition. Science is best when honest scientists, some wanting to prove the guess and others wanting to disprove the guess, work together to discover the truth. Science is very exact. There is no room in science for democracy. If a guess can be disproven, then it is invalid. That doesn't negate what has been observed. However, the scientific method will lead to a reformulation of the guess and further experimentation and observation.

Perversion is not the result of science, but the idea put forth by ungodly scientists that science can somehow disprove the existence of God. If anything, science should lead to a better understanding of God since the object of science, all that is visible, clearly reflects His power and nature, according to Paul.

Perversion can happen in every arena of life,

and the progression is always the same. The first step is replacing God.

The first experiment in government didn't happen in the late eighteenth century on the continent named after Italian explorer and map-maker Amerigo Vespucci. God's people, centuries ago, had no king even though all the other nations they knew about had kings. God ruled His people directly and worked through prophets and judges that He Himself had chosen.

Around 1100 BC, Samuel, a judge in Israel, was getting very old. The people were afraid he was going to die and leave his wicked sons in charge, so they asked him to choose a king to take his place so that they could be like everyone else in the world. The people didn't think it was a bad idea. Samuel's sons weren't fair; they were greedy and also accepted bribes. The people reasoned that everyone else had a king and seemed to be doing OK. Samuel, however, was immediately upset. He knew that the people were rejecting God. Step one toward perversion was in the works; God was replaced by a human king.

With man in charge, his understanding of God's Word drifted away from the truth. One of Jesus' major headaches during His ministry was contending with the misconceptions of the religious leaders at the time. After Jesus' death, the confusion propagated by those religious leaders only multiplied.

Step two didn't happen for a couple of thousand years. The "Enlightenment" was beginning, and people were having their eyes opened. The colonies of various European powers, in the course of their human events, decided that the kings across the sea were evil and they wanted a new and safer form of government: a government of the people, for the people, and by the people. It sounded really good.

God was replaced by a king, and the king was replaced by a new concept in government, the rule of law. Today, the god of the United States is the US Constitution. Right and wrong, good and bad, are determined by its articles and amendments. Judges are its bishops, and lawyers are its priests. The one true God and His direction are outside of its scope and therefore irrelevant. It follows that no religion is more important or more correct or incorrect in the eyes of the law. The law, and ultimately the Constitution, is god.

As the perversion continues, there is no room for God or faith within the US government. It sounds good. How can we be fair to the adherents of the many religions that have come to America seeking refuge and safety if we don't tolerate and respect their religion? How can we expect other countries to do the same for our citizens? But the result is evil. Instead of God directing man according to His plan and purpose, now we have man attempting to tell God what is right and wrong according to his own whims.

There is no problem with law when it comes from God. When the nation of Israel was first established, God gave them laws. Later, the New Testament explained that the law was a temporary measure to lead the nation into an obedient relationship with Christ. When the people back in Samuel's day rejected God from being their King, He didn't quit or give up on them.

If a man follows God, the law becomes irrelevant because, in following God, he will obey all the laws. Laws are still necessary for men who make themselves out to be their own god. In that respect, governments are the servants of God, rewarding those who do the right thing and punishing the immoral. A government that fails to protect its people fails in its moral obligation to God. A government that tries to protect its people without looking to God for guidance is doomed to fail.

When a government sets itself up to be higher than God, it is no better than either the man who proclaims he is a god or Satan, the one who originally attempted to usurp the throne of God. Governments are made up of men who have limited understanding and are compelled by self-seeking hearts.

An excellent illustration of how America has drifted away from God and moved man into the position of authority can be seen in the presidential proclamations of Thanksgiving Day. The early proclamations, such as those given by George Washington or Abraham Lincoln, speak of the nation's utter dependence on the benevolent, almighty God. There can be no misunderstanding that our original congress and those early presidents understood that God to be the Judeo-Christian God. More recent proclamations, mindful of the Constitution and Supreme Court decisions, take into account that Americans worship many different gods and thus proclaim that everyone should be thankful in whatever way they choose and be respectful of people that recognize no god at all.

Lot and Sodom

Terah was the great, great, great, great, great, great, great grandson of Noah and lived in a little town called Ur in the Chaldean region of the world. He had three sons, Abram, Nahor, and Haran. All three sons got married. Haran and his wife had a son named Lot while Abram's wife, Sarai, couldn't have children. Perhaps it was the premature death of Haran that motivated Terah to leave Ur and move to Canaan with Abram, Sarai, and Lot.

Terah never made it to Canaan. He and his son, daughter-in-law and grandson made it as far as Charan and settled down there. Terah died in Charan. In the meantime, Abram and Lot, his nephew, became wealthy.

God spoke to Abram and told him to get moving again, so he, Sarai, and Lot left Charan and eventually landed in Canaan.

The herds of Abram and Lot were so large that their shepherds competed for pastures. Abram finally told Lot they needed to separate. He told Lot to pick where he wanted to settle and he would choose a different place. Lot chose the area around the Jordan River after he noticed how rich with green grass it was. In the far south of the area was the land of Sodom, a land with its own king, full of wicked men.

Lot was identified with Sodom well enough that when Sodom and its allies were defeated in a war, Lot was taken captive along with the rest of the inhabitants. Later, after Abram came to his rescue, Lot became one of the leading residents of the land, sitting in judgment of the people. That may have ensued on account of his wealth since the men of the city resented an outsider having so much authority.

Though Lot chose the valley of the Jordan for selfish reasons, he maintained his integrity before God while he lived among wicked men.

The Sin of Sodom and America

A common misunderstanding is that the sin of Sodom was sodomy. Sodomy was only the symptom of the sin.

In the sixteenth chapter of Ezekiel, God is harshly scolding and warning Jerusalem about its actions and rebellion. During the course of the rebuke, He says they are worse than Sodom and her sisters (Gomorrah, Admah, and Zeboiim) and goes on to explain the fourfold sin of Sodom.

Sodom was arrogant. She thought she was better than anyone else.

Sodom was stuffed with food. She had plenty to eat and ate her fill.

Sodom had plenty of free time. She had no threat or imposition coming against her.

Sodom did nothing to sustain or support the poor and the downcast.

The symptoms of their sin played out in their attitudes and actions. In their arrogance, they committed abominations (*toe'ayvah*). God watched for so long, and then eliminated them like a surgeon eliminates a cancerous tumor.

America is arrogant. Its arrogance is evident in its actions. More than any other country, the

United States tells the rest of the world what to do. Even though it is only one of hundreds of sovereign nations in the world, it treats the rest of the world with contempt. That would not be the case if it held certain standards and lived up to the standards it enforces on the rest of the world. But the United States lives by one set of rules and enforces another set on everyone else. America thinks it's different. America thinks it's better. The rest of the world doesn't understand.

Any nation that tries to assert its own national sovereignty in contrast to America's wishes soon feels the weight of the world's superpower bully. America forces its will on the rest of the world, beginning with international name calling, escalating to different types of sanctions as severe as forcing the nation into poverty, and culminating in actual military intervention. Very few countries can stand up to America and get away with it.

The arrogance of America on the world stage is also reflected by individual Americans. American tourists who visit other lands expect special treatment. They expect to get away with breaking the laws in other nations as a matter of course, since the only laws that really matter to them are American laws. They expect that the rights granted by the Constitution are theirs to assert, worldwide. And if they are arrested in another land, they expect the U.S. government to come to their rescue.

Most countries with heritages much older than America's brush off the brutish pride of this young upstart nation and do enough to stay on its good side. Many countries foster a deep hatred for the United States based on its pride and the actions that flow out of it. That hatred is multiplied because of America's deceptive ways and the underhanded tactics it uses in order to secure its own interests.

This is not new. The United States has not changed its behavior toward the rest of the world for as long as most people who are now alive can remember. From time to time individuals try to make a change, but the nation is suffering from a perverse sickness that only God can heal.

Americans are self-centered; many Christians honestly believe that the true church is alive only in America. A group of young people from a Christian college in Texas went to Southeast Asia on a mission trip over their spring break. What surprised most of them was the fact that Christian churches with fervently believing, Christ-following members were already there. In fact, the Christian church is stronger in many places outside America. It should be noted here that Lot's presence did not save Sodom.

In the Land of the Free, some of the things that became sin for Sodom are counted among God's blessings. Americans construe freedom as having a God given right to do whatever they want. The Declaration of Independence promoted that misperception when it proclaimed that life, liberty, and the pursuit of happiness are God given rights. It looks good and sounds right, though.

God expects His people to be a conduit of blessing. Clearly, having enough to eat is a blessing from God. It is counted among His blessings in more than one passage of scripture.

Even so, people who have plenty to eat have food to share. Samaria was in a similar condition to Sodom in that respect when Amos condemned them for the same sin of which Sodom was guilty: stuffing their faces and oppressing the poor. He called the women of Samaria cows and said God would drag them away with fishhooks.

America is stuffed with food. Today, the World Health Organization reports that the United States has the highest obesity rate of any country. Is America acting like Samaria and Sodom?

The Bible belt is an informal label for that area in the United States where evangelical Christianity permeates the culture. The Centers for Disease Control and Prevention report that over a third of Americans are obese with the highest concentrations of obesity in the Bible belt. According to the US Census Bureau, the Bible belt is also the area with the highest concentration of Americans in poverty.

We sin due to our frail human nature. One of the strongest rebukes Paul levied against the church was directed at wealthy Christians who, when the church met together, ate their fill to the point that the poor went hungry. In America, Christians are following in the footsteps of the church at Corinth. Instead of being a beacon of light, the part of the country most noted for its Christianity is leading the way in the second aspect of the sin of Sodom, namely, having plenty of food but eating all of it themselves.

One of the greatest blessings in the Bible and part of the reward to the faithful is rest. Free time can be a major contributor to rest so it may be difficult to understand why free time is included in the sin of Sodom. To gain a proper perspective, it is important to understand that free time, like food, is a God given resource. Free time can be wasted and ill-used just like any other resource.

God is not a hard task master who drives His followers to exhaustion. Jesus said His yoke was easy and His load was light. The way He conducted His ministry is an example of how God expects us to act. He never raced around from place to place trying to do too much. He and His disciples set out in a direction and arrived when they got there. He taught about the nature and instructions of God as He went along the way and dealt with people's questions, problems, and needs as they came up. His ministry illustrates what Paul taught when he told us to do the good works God had already prepared for us. The Christian life is not meant to be difficult. A Christian must simply learn, trust, listen, and obey. God takes care of the remainder.

When Jesus got tired, He rested. Sometimes He withdrew with His disciples, sometimes He went off by Himself. His agenda was the will of God, and He received updates in real time. If we are prepared with God's word and tuned in to His Spirit, ministry will flow through us as we go about conducting our lives day to day. God has already arranged the opportunities.

America has plenty of free time. The average American has about five and a half hours of free time a day according to the latest report from the US Bureau of Labor Statistics. Of that, they spend nearly three hours a day watching television, about 45 minutes socializing, and about half an hour exercising or playing sports. Virtually every American has a few extra minutes to spend throughout the day doing the will of God; in particular, taking care of those God is most concerned about, namely, the poor, the widowed, and the orphaned.

The fourth part of Sodom's sin gets to the heart of the matter. They failed to take care of their poor. Another way of translating the phrase in Ezekiel is they failed to empower the powerless. It's not as if they didn't have the resources or the time, but their pride blinded them to the plight of the needy.

The United States started off on the wrong foot. The founding fathers, by their own rationale, were rejecting the idea of divine leadership through a monarch and replacing it with self-rule justified by certain "inalienable" God given rights. That the Declaration of Independence refers to the God of the Bible is clear from the words, "endowed by their Creator." But none of the rights claimed by the Declaration of Independence is supported in scripture.

A right is only as good as the grantor's ability to enforce it. An individual can assert his own rights if he has enough power. The rights Americans enjoy are granted and enforced by their government. If and when the government changes its mind or ceases to enforce a right, it disappears. But any right granted by God does not need man to enforce it. He is powerful and sufficiently capable of enforcing the rights He grants to His people.

There are only two rights explicitly granted in scripture; both are mentioned by John. In the first chapter of John's gospel we learn that anyone who receives Jesus, believes in the power of His name, and is born again by His power has a right to become a child of God. In the last chapter of the book of Revelation we learn that those who obey Jesus will have a right to eat the fruit from the tree of life by virtue of the fact that their sins are forgiven.

The rights claimed in the Declaration of Independence are actually antithetical to what the scripture teaches.

First of all, life belongs to God. No one can give life, and no individual has the right to take it away. It is a gift from God that He can take away at any time He sees fit. It is out of that reality that scripture teaches us to respect life.

It's clear from scripture that Christians place Christ before their own life. According to Luke 14, that must happen in order to become a Christian in the first place. Paul, at the end of 1st Corinthians 6, says that Christians don't own their own lives but have been bought with the blood of Jesus.

But what about the unbelievers? Do they own their own life? In Luke 12, when a man asks Jesus to tell his brother to divide the inheritance, Jesus responds to the request with a warning against envy. He gives an example of a wealthy individual who has managed to set aside a hefty retirement. The individual decided to take it easy and party since he had enough to live on for many years. But before he could enjoy any of his hard earned treasure, God took his life. It was his time for reckoning.

In Ezekiel 18 God proclaims that He owns everyone. As the owner of everyone, He alone sits in judgment. It is in this passage that He emphatically declares that the one who commits a sin will die. The only grounds on which man can claim a right to life is sinless perfection. The fact that people die every day is proof that everyone in the world gives up the right to life as a consequence of their sin, regardless of what the American Declaration of Independence might say.

To be sure, the scripture makes it clear that God is the source of life. He is also the strongest supporter of life in every respect. Life at every level is also a sign of God's involvement in the world. It is so important to Him that He manages it personally. He does not grant the right of life or delegate the responsibility for life to man.

Christians have erroneously carried over this falsely proclaimed God given right to life in their effort to stem the tide of abortion. Abortion is wrong, not because the unborn child has a God given right to live, but because God has reserved the right to life and, except in situations He has specifically given direction, no person or government on earth has a right to take the life of another person, whether it is before or after they are born.

The Declaration also claims the God given right to liberty. In order to address the claim, the concept of liberty, or freedom, must be understood. Liberty means to have the ability, authority, or permission to do something, but liberty only has meaning within some sort of context. None of the founding fathers imagined the right of liberty to imply that permission to murder was included in the definition.

Paul devotes chapters six through eight of his letter to the Romans to the subject of freedom. In chapter six he says that men have a choice as to which master they follow. They can choose to follow God through Jesus, or they can follow their own desires. Either choice results in freedom and slavery. A person who follows Christ is His slave but is set free by His power from the destructive power of sin. On the other hand, a person who follows his own desires becomes a slave to his passion and effectively lives free from the law of God. God calls men to obedience. He does not release them to do whatever they want.

A people who follow Christ will live in harmony because He is orchestrating their actions. A people who follow their own appetites struggle to live in peace because no one is in charge, thus they all pull in different directions. The truth of the principle is easy to see in marriages today. A husband and wife who follow Christ will forgive each other when they don't feel like it, for example, out of obedience to their Lord. Godless couples will stay together as long as they want the same things. They separate after they have "grown apart" enough, or when one decides that something different would be better.

The right to liberty as claimed in the Declaration of Independence is interpreted to mean that Americans can do whatever they want. "It's a free country." The only boundaries on American freedom are the laws rooted in the Constitution. It's interesting to note that even with a perverted sense of what liberty means, America allowed, in contradiction to the Declaration of Independence, rich men to own poor men as property. But then, the government of the United States has always found a way to legally justify whatever it wanted to do. After all, "It's a free country."

Unbridled liberty can have only one of two end results. People who have liberty from evil are controlled from within by the Spirit of God and will be the conduit of life to others. People who have liberty as the Declaration of Independence is presently interpreted must be controlled by an exterior set of laws. As the law changes and exerts less and less control over those that need to be controlled, they become conduits of death, both spiritually and physically, to others around them. Control through humanly devised and hence perverse laws results in perverse outcomes.

God has not granted a right to liberty in any temporal sense of the word. 1st Corinthians seven is one of the New Testament passages that touch on slavery. In the course of making the point that someone shouldn't try to force a change in his external conditions due to becoming a Christian, Paul remarks that a slave who becomes a Christian shouldn't care about being a slave. Paul goes on to say that one should become free if given the opportunity, but being a slave shouldn't be the issue.

The Bible records the arrests of Paul, Peter,

and even Jesus. In every case something good and powerful resulted from the imprisoned person accepting his situation as the will of God. Paul's letter to Philemon was written to pave the way for the return of his slave, Onesimus. Paul was in prison when he wrote the letter. The reason none of those arrested demanded a God given right to liberty or claimed false imprisonment was because no such right exists. They accepted their circumstances in the course of their obedience and prayed to God for understanding.

Men can't predict the future and have no idea what effect their present circumstances will have on their life or the lives of others, and yet they spend so much effort trying to change them. One source of invaluable peace is submitting to the providence of God in situations when liberty is scarce, instead of claiming and fighting for some errant right.

The claim of the right to pursue happiness makes it clear that the world would be happy if God would just shut up and go away. Of the rights claimed in the Declaration of Independence, the right to pursue happiness is the most blatant in conflict with scripture. Jesus told His disciples that they would be hated on account of following Him. Peter said that Jesus showed us the way to a better life through His suffering, and we should follow His example. Paul said that one of the highest goals in his life was to know Jesus by suffering the way He suffered.

It's not that God intends for His people, or the rest of the world, to be miserable, but misery is an excellent teacher. The average person tends to forget God when everything is going well. Tragedy tends to put things back in focus. A man who has never been hungry is less likely to understand or have compassion for people who are always hungry. A woman who has always had something comfortable and fashionable to wear is less likely to understand or have compassion for people who can only occasionally buy something from a second-hand store, or who can't afford to buy any clothes at all.

John goes so far as to say that God is love. He illustrated His compassion for us by sending His only Son. What He wants the world to experience transcends happiness. Joy is a gift from God that is not dependent on the circumstances. Peter and Paul were able to sing while they were chained up in crude prisons, not because they were happy with their immediate circumstances, but because their relationship with God through Jesus filled them with joy. Joy is not available by decree or by right. It is, however, freely and immediately accessible to anyone who has faith in and is willing to submit to the will of God.

The rights claimed in the Declaration of Independence sound good and look right. But they put the nation in the wrong mindset from the start. They set the stage for selfishness on a national level. With such a flawed beginning, it's easy to see how America has slipped further away from God into perversion.

In the early 60's, it became illegal to pray in school based on a Supreme Court decision regarding religious liberty. The ruling was based on the concept of separation of church and state first mentioned by Thomas Jefferson. The first amendment, however, was added to keep a secular government out of the affairs of the church. European nations had a related problem in which their governments were essentially run by a particular church thereby imposing official governmental influence on any other church not officially recognized. The original intent of the amendment was not to separate the government from church but to prevent one church from persecuting another. Since its inclusion in the Constitution, the first amendment has been turned on its head to prevent any church from having any influence in government. The end result is a nation of people slipping farther and farther from God and focused more and more on their own selfish ambitions.

Think about the law in America to further understand how she could find herself with the perverted outlook of Sodom. Law originates from God. The first law, given to Adam, was to avoid eating the fruit from the tree of the knowledge of good and evil. Intertwined within all laws is the concept of right and wrong. The prohibition to Adam was not given because God wanted to keep him in the dark. God wanted to direct him. By eating the forbidden fruit, man took it upon himself to decide right from wrong instead of relying on the superior understanding and wisdom of God.

As God's instrument, governments are responsible to Him to enforce right and wrong. But when a government rejects God, it must find an ungodly basis of right and wrong. In America, the majority get to pick what's right and wrong. As a result, what is legal in America is not necessarily what is right in God's eyes. As further proof of the principle, what is illegal today may be legal tomorrow based on the notions of five people living in Washington DC.

Over time, powerful men with lots of money bribed, coerced, and brainwashed a nation of self-absorbed, self-centered sheep to vote their way. Hence, things that were clearly wrong, shameful, and unthinkable in the past, in due course became acceptable. Men, no matter how powerful or rich, obviously don't live long enough to preside over the centuries-long slide into moral decay. But the serpent who was in the Garden of Eden is still coaxing men to take an even bigger bite of the fruit God warned against. Good and evil have never been a matter for man to decide.

The land of the free and home of the brave is ruled by fear and greed. The same revered fountain of wisdom who avowed that there should be "a wall of separation" between church and state, also proclaimed that there is no place for sports in institutions of higher learning. Try getting any major American college to buy that line. In that instance, Thomas Jefferson didn't understand the issue. There's just too much profit in football and the love of money will find a way to prevail over principles every time. Americans get to choose what they want to believe and what's right and wrong. They worry about the justification afterward.

Does America support the poor or sustain the downcast as Sodom failed to do?

In the United States, one out of every five households is below the government determined poverty line. At the same time, the average net worth of a U.S. congressman is in the neighborhood of four million dollars. Most congressmen don't have the faintest idea what it really means to be poor. It's hard for someone to sympathize with what they don't understand.

While a significant number of Americans skip meals because they can't afford to eat, 400 American billionaires go about their day to day business. A billion dollars rationed out at $100,000 a year, a substantial income even by American standards, would last 5,000 years - thousands of years longer than the longest lived empires of the world. The 20 richest men in America combined are worth well over a trillion dollars. That's the equivalent of every man, woman and child in the country giving over $3,000 to 20 men.

Even the poorest people in America would be considered rich in many countries. The implication in Ezekiel 16, nevertheless, is that Sodom was neglecting the poor in Sodom. The human tendency in charity is to look beyond our borders to help the poor starving children in Africa and Asia. That inclination is related to the fact Jesus made in remark when He noted that prophets held no honor in their home town among people who knew them. The poor among us are left to fend for themselves. Here, it's every man for himself. Not necessarily out of maliciousness, but we become acclimated and indifferent to what we are accustomed to. We are not as concerned about the poor who will always be with us.

But God isn't keeping score of the number of poor people that His children help. The outlook that causes a man to ignore someone in need reveals the condition of his heart. If there is no compassion toward the needy person who is living or working or walking nearby, then the dollars sent overseas are probably not motivated by compassion either. This is illustrated in 1st John 4 which says a man can't hate his brother that he sees and relates to on a daily basis and then claim to love God whom he has never seen. The attitude which will keep people from slipping into perversion is revealed through their face to face interaction with others.

The Christian church in America is an equal party to the national frame of mind. How many churches with multi-million dollar buildings will help a struggling church in a poor neighborhood if they are unrelated, such as a church from a different denomination? How many churches are focused on their own well-being or their political or worldly influence? How many cups of cold water have been given by Christians with no strings attached or expectations of any kind simply because they saw a need?

It's far too common for churches in America to minister only in circumstances where they will get something in return, even if it's only a boost in reputation. If the church fails to follow the example Christ set, how can it hope to be an example to a dying nation.

Ezekiel 16 is a prophecy against Judah. Sodom and its sins were mentioned as a way of explanation to show Judah how they had surpassed Sodom in its wickedness. Judah's sin, as Sodom's, started with idolatry: taking their eyes off God.

In the name of freedom, America has become the most perverse, self-centered nation on earth. For decades, America has celebrated the importation of wickedness from every corner of the globe. It is to the point that countries America considered wicked in days gone by now sit as her judges. The contrast can be seen, for example, in places where overseas U.S. military bases have closed. Small cities near those bases in Europe had thriving "Red Light" districts where prostitution and the sex trade flourished. After the Americans left, the sex trade disappeared. Even in larger cities, sex districts that thrived on American business presently barely exist.

In her perverted state, the United States has become double-minded. On one hand, for example, it uses policy and sanctions to force other nations to uphold human rights while secretly condoning and practicing the same types of abuse it condemns publicly. We preach our own purity while we export filth.

Paul told Timothy that the time would come when people would not tolerate what truth teaches. He said men would find professors of fables that would repeat what they want to hear. That time for America is now.

"A dog barks and stands at bay if he sees anyone assault his master. I would surely be negligent, if, seeing the truth of God thus attacked, I should remain dumb, without giving one hint of warning."

- John Calvin

HOMOSEXUALITY

Homosexual Behavior is a Sin

It is important to understand the distinction between temptation and behavior.

Temptation, or the enticement to sin, is an assault, though it is hardly ever recognized as such. It can come from many places. The one who brings temptation always has a motive, or the answer to the question, "What's in it for me?" When the devil tempted Jesus, he took advantage of His weakened condition. The devil's motive was to assure his own continued reign by putting an end to Jesus' ministry and dragging Him to hell.

The devil is not the only source of temptation. Temptation can come from people as well, arising out of their own motives. Most often, temptation comes from our own desires. An old beer commercial tapped into that truth by proclaiming that we only have one life to live, so live with all the zest possible before it's all over. In scripture, James points out the fact that men are tempted by their own desires and never by God.

Some people don't even try to resist temptation. They follow the words of Horace, the ancient Latin poet, who coined the phrase, "Carpe diem," which loosely translated means live for today.

One of the assurances we have that Jesus can empathize with the plight of our humanity is the fact that He was tempted in every way that we are. The passage in Hebrews 4 that draws attention to Jesus' vulnerability also points out that He never sinned, in spite of the temptation. Jesus demonstrated that there is no limit to the amount of temptation that we can resist.

Sin does not happen until a person responds by giving in through action to the temptation to do something wrong. Take, for example, a person who gets cut off while driving down a highway. He may have an immediate emotional response of anger. The anger grows into the motivation to get revenge. Anger and vengeance become the temptation to do something. At any moment, the person's brain can intervene and offer the alternative; forgiveness. The person has a choice to make. If he acts in vengeance through retaliation or gesture, or even calling the offender a fool, he has crossed the line into sin.

Homosexual behavior is explicitly prohibited in the 18th chapter of Leviticus. The chapter prohibits several sexual sins including adultery, incest, bestiality, and homosexuality. The reason these sins are mentioned in the law at all is because they were all being practiced in the region, and various individuals within the congregation of Israel were tempted by these things.

Homosexual behavior is not new or modern. It has been practiced for thousands of years. God enlightened His people and told them it was a sin that should be avoided.

Sexual Perversion

Perversion starts with temptation and moves through an outrageous, deceptively false conclusion, based on an accepted premise. When the devil tempted Jesus in the wilderness, he began with the accepted premise, "If you are the Son of God..." The false conclusion was, "Turn these stones into bread." Jesus knew He was the Son of God and caught the trick in the temptation. He did not have to turn stones into bread to prove He was the Son of God. Turning stones to bread was within Jesus' power, but it was a perverted way to satisfy His hunger. Jesus knew He was to rely on His Father and chose instead to stay hungry for a while.

Those involved in the counter-culture revolution of the 60's rebelled against stereotypes of all kinds including the stereotyped roles of men and women. Stereotyping is certainly wrong and is a major contributor to prejudice. That is a true and generally accepted premise. Just because stereotyping is wrong, however, does not mean every conclusion drawn from that truth is also true. Little boys play with toy soldiers which are essentially a form of doll. The stereotyping of little boys by forcing them to avoid playing with girls' dolls became an issue that was popularly demonized by the movement. The deceptively false conclusion that some little boys secretly want to be little girls, however, was and is perverse.

Sexuality is a biologically determined reality. It is biologically impossible, according to nature, for a human female to be trapped inside a male body or a human male to be trapped inside a female body. A male is incapable of bearing a child and a female is incapable of fertilizing a human egg. No amount of cosmetics, hormone therapy or surgery can change that.

A male pretending to be a female is one of the biblical definitions of perversion. Then again, just because a girl likes to climb trees, play baseball and is good in science doesn't mean she is really a boy. Letting her climb trees, play baseball and pursue her chosen career field should not be a threat to her sexuality. God created everyone unique for many reasons, but each in their own uniqueness is either male or female.

What the Bible Says

The Bible first mentions homosexual behavior in Genesis 18 and 19. The fact that two chapters are dedicated to the subject this early in the Bible is an indication of its importance. All of history prior to the flood is encapsulated in the first five chapters. The next six chapters are devoted to the flood, Noah, and his family. The story of Lot and Sodom is interjected right in the middle of the next 12 chapters which are devoted to Abraham.

In Genesis 18, God sends angels to investigate what is going on in Sodom. On the way, they stop to see Abraham and tell him he will have a son. They also explain to him that they are investigating a loud distress call coming from Sodom and Gomorrah arising out of incredibly heavy guilt.

Abraham must have known what was going on because he immediately assumed they were going to destroy the cities even though the angels made no mention of judgment. He begins pleading for mercy for as few as ten innocent people who may be living there.

An interesting question to ponder is the source of the anguished cry.

Was it the soul of Lot crying out? Lot had been with Abraham since the family had left Ur in the Chaldean region. He was rescued by Abraham when Sodom was defeated and taken into captivity by its greedy neighbors. The only ill word spoken of him was the fact that he selfishly chose the best land when his uncle, Abraham, gave him the choice. It's possible that Lot's prayers and the imperceptible groaning of his soul was the source of the cry.

Perhaps the source of the cry was the land Sodom was built upon. There are other examples of the land crying out to God recorded in the Bible. God told Cain that the voice of his murdered brother, Abel, was crying out to Him from the ground. When the Pharisees told Jesus to silence the crowd during the triumphal entry into Jerusalem, He told them that if the multitudes ceased to praise Him, the stones would begin to shout. Possibly the land of Sodom had endured all it could bear.

Maybe the source of the cry was the collective voice of the victims of the grievous sins being perpetrated. The agents of violence act with self-centered motives and perspective with callous disregard for the needs and feelings of others. Sometimes crying out to God is the only recourse left to the victim. The angels didn't divulge where the cry originated. They only say that God had heard it and was responding.

When God's messengers arrived in Sodom they initially turned down Lot's hospitality and planned to spend the night in the city's plaza. Lot definitely knew what was going on in the city; so he vigorously persuaded them to stay in his house.

Before bedtime, men and boys from all over the city encircled Lot's house. They asked Lot to turn his visitors out so they could gang rape them. Lot came out and pleaded with them to refrain from carrying out their wicked intention. Coincidently, the Aramaic word used for wicked, *ra'a*, also means to make a loud noise.

The state of perversion that the men of Sodom had stooped to is evident in these verses. In order to protect his guests, Lot offers them his two virgin daughters to do with as they pleased, but they threatened him with worse treatment than they had planned for his visitors.

The angels had all the proof they needed and arranged to destroy the city promptly. Ezekiel 16 explains that the men of Sodom committed abominations, and God removed them when He saw it.

All of this happened before the realization of

the covenant. Isaac had not even been born yet. It happened before the law was given. The fact that the men of Sodom were held accountable for their sin is an illustration of the words Paul wrote in the first chapter of Romans, specifically, that there is never an excuse for sin. The revelation of guilt in these early chapters of Genesis affirms Paul's proclamation that men have understood the nature, character, and power of God since the beginning of creation. Abraham and Lot both knew without the benefit of the law that the men of Sodom were immoral.

Centuries later, when Moses delivered God's law to His people, an edict against homosexual behavior was included. In Leviticus chapter 18 it specifically says, "With a male you will not lie down in place of lying down with a woman. That is an abomination." The word used for abomination here is, *Toe'ayvah*.

It's not as if God was trying to come up with things to put in the law. The chapter begins the same way the Ten Commandments begin; with God reminding his people that He is Yahweh, their God. The chapter is a warning and prohibition against the evil that they were already aware of since it was going on in Egypt, and the depraved behavior thcy would later discover was also a way of life in the land of Canaan, to which God was leading them. Addressing many of those customs, the chapter also prohibits incest, bestiality, adultery, and child sacrifice.

Toward the end of the chapter, Moses cautions that ignoring God's direction would result in several consequences. First, they would be thrown off the land in the same way as the people they were going to dispossess. Second, they would be cut off from their own people. And finally, they would be tainted in the eyes of God.

It's popular among the proponents of homosexuality to dismiss what the Bible says about it as outdated Old Testament laws that do not apply today or as antiquated cultural norms that have not kept up with the times. The New Testament, in fact, addresses that issue. Dietary laws in particular, of which a violation in the Old Testament was an abomination, were changed. There is no indication anywhere in scripture, however, that God has changed the way he feels about homosexuality, incest, bestiality, adultery, or child sacrifice.

The New Testament has several passages that address homosexual behavior and make it clear that it continues to be an abomination in the sight of God.

Beginning in the first chapter of Romans, Paul makes the case that explains man's depravity and the need for salvation through Jesus. He makes it clear that there are no exceptions, either in the area of man's immorality, or in God's expectations. To begin the argument, he illustrates how people progress from a state of knowing God to a state of total corruption. Toward the end of the slide into total perversion, he says that God allows people to indulge in disgraceful or revolting situations in which women trade natural sex for something outside of the natural, and men reject natural sex with women and burn with lust for other men, "*arsenes en arsesin.*" But God also guarantees that they will individually receive a just settlement for their actions. Those who believe homosexuality is alright with God are in genuine danger of blasphemy against the Holy Spirit.

People at that stage of perversion have rejected God and His wisdom. The next step in the process is a failed mind, to pursue whatever corruption they please. In other words, He writes them off in the same way he rejected those who were dissuaded from following Him into the Promised Land when ten of the spies brought back a disconcerting report. (See the book of Numbers chapters 13 and 14.) He writes them off the same way He wrote off the people of Judah when He told Jeremiah to stop praying for the people since He was not listening because they had committed all types of sin and carried on in the temple as if nothing had happened. He allowed them to be captured and held hostage for decades by the king of Babylon. (See Jeremiah chapter seven.)

Paul also addresses homosexual behavior in his letters to the Corinthians. Corinth was a coastal town next to an isthmus in southern Greece about 40 miles west of Athens and 70 miles northeast of Sparta. The church at Corinth had a vibrant, exciting, and passionate congregation. They exercised the gifts of the Spirit, met regularly to celebrate the Lord's Supper, and welcomed the apostle with open arms. Some of the members of the Corinthian church also had the most bizarre problems mentioned in the New Testament, and Paul was constantly admonishing them.

In the sixth chapter of Paul's first letter to

Corinth, he tells them that the unjust will not have any part of the kingdom or power of God. Beginning in the ninth verse, he lists ten different lifestyles that will alienate God. They are male prostitutes, idolaters, adulterers, catamites, homosexuals, embezzlers, greedy people, drunks, revilers, and robbers.

He goes on to say that the issue with these things is not whether they are legal or not. The issue is the state of the temple wherein the Holy Spirit is living since the body of a Christian is the temple of the Holy Spirit. Just because something is legal does not make it a good idea. Let's take being drunk as an example. While it is illegal to drive while intoxicated and being inebriated will exacerbate a disorderly conduct arrest, it is perfectly legal to sit at home and stay drunk. It's not healthy, robs an individual of self-control, eliminates a person's emotional control, prevents any meaningful chance of being productive, and stands a good chance of damaging close relationships, to say nothing of the harmful effects to one's health, but it is legal.

Everything on the list is forgivable. It's not the individual acts that alienate God and keep the offender out of His kingdom but rather the perverted mentality of the one that makes excuses within his own thoughts and condones the constant repetition, and rationalizes that these acts are not sinful or offensive to God.

Three out of the ten immoral habits on Paul's list have to do with homosexuality. Those who practiced homosexuality did not hide and were not ashamed of their lifestyle; it was a cultural norm. Paul instructed Christians to remain free and avoid the custom.

The first on the list is the Greek word *pornos*. It is the masculine form of *pornē*, which means prostitute or harlot. It is sometimes translated with the more broad meaning of fornication from the implication of the word which is sex for the sake of sex. While it is possible that on a rare occasion a woman would employ a male prostitute, most of the customers were men looking to relieve themselves with no scruples or inhibitions concerning the object of relief. Paul says here that men who prostitute themselves will not see heaven or enjoy the protections and rewards of the Kingdom of God while they live.

In ancient Greece, prostitutes (*pornē*) would draw pictures and write (*grapho*) things on the walls of their bedrooms in order to help their johns perform when they were unable. That is the origin and source of the word "pornography" (*pornē/grapho*). Some of the best preserved archeological examples of this can be found in the ruins of Pompeii, a city that was completely buried by the volcano Vesuvius in a span of about 6 hours and totally forgotten until it was accidentally found by construction workers about 1500 years later.

Paul also includes catamites (*malakos*) on the list. The word literally means soft or smooth and in that sense is used of young boys kept by older men for the purpose of having sex. The practice of having and using catamites (homosexual pedophilia) was common in both ancient Greece and the Roman Empire and consequently, the first Christians were aware of the custom. It was accepted as a type of rite of passage. Many men in positions of power and authority not only kept catamites, but had been catamites themselves until they reached the age of manhood. This may be the starkest example in all of ancient culture as how Christians were different and set apart from the world in which they lived. Again, Paul said that men who persisted in that type of life would be rejected by God and would ultimately be forgotten by Him.

The third lifestyle Paul includes on the list is homosexuals (*arsenokoites*). The Greek word is actually two words put together. The same thing happens in English (sunrise, breakfast, football). The Greek word, *arseno* is the word for man, as in male (in Latin – *homo*). The Greek word for man, as in "mankind", is *anthropos*, though like the English word, it can also be used to refer to the male. Jesus used it that way in Matthew 19:5. The Greek word, *koite* is directly related to the English word, "coitus" and has the same meaning. "Homosexual" is actually a polite translation of the Greek *arsenokoites*. Paul could not have said more graphically or with less uncertainty that homosexuals violate God's justice, are sinful, and will have no part in God's kingdom. They live in and spread deception.

Time and again, Christians are warned in the New Testament to shun strange teachings and hold fast to Jesus and His doctrines. Homosexuality is the pinnacle of deception and Satan's ultimate victory over man. It is man's strongest rebellion against God, in effect, shaking a clenched fist with an iron will of disobedience and rejection.

Paul similarly speaks about homosexuality in

his first letter to his disciple, Timothy. He begins by warning him to avoid myths and to refrain from getting bogged down in the "begats" of the Old Testament. He also encourages him to remember the reason why he is where he is. He had a duty to teach God's law so the members of the church would have a godly love for each other that flows from a pure heart, a clear conscience, and a sincere faith. He warns that any other use of the law will pervert its purpose. God's word is the only course to a pure heart, a clear conscience, and a sincere faith.

Out of that perspective, Paul goes on to say that the law didn't come about for the sake of God fearing, upright men such as Abraham and Job. God instituted the law because so many people were running in the opposite direction, hurting each other and committing abominations.

For a better understanding of the rationale for laws consider the seatbelt law. Laws making the use of seatbelts mandatory would have never been necessary if everyone wore seatbelts in the first place. But since so many drivers preferred to risk being maimed and killed in an accident as opposed to the inconvenience of wearing a seatbelt, laws had to be passed. A government's first responsibility is the physical protection of its citizens.

In the beginning of his first letter to Timothy, Paul lists many types of people that the law was made for, though the last item on the list is a catch all for anything opposed to God's sound teaching which he might have failed to point out. Included on this list, as in the letter to Corinth, are male prostitutes and homosexuals. It's interesting that he lists homicide, matricide, and patricide separately.

Born That Way

A popular argument for the acceptance of homosexuality is that some men are born homosexual. They should not be judged or reviled for simply being who they are and who they were born to be.

It is clear throughout scripture that man is born with a sinful nature. That does not mean, however, that God holds them accountable for the sins committed by their ancestors. Ezekiel chapter 18 addresses that common misperception and makes it clear that God holds every man accountable exclusively for his own sins.

A person's nature determines his character and disposition. There is no question that some men are born homosexual. Some are natural born liars. Others are born inherently lazy. All are born selfish.

The nature of something is the essence of what it creates or the actions it takes. There are several examples in scripture that illustrate this principle. In Proverbs, to illustrate that a fool will always act foolishly, Solomon compares him to the dog that eats its own vomit. There is no amount of training that will prevent the dog from wanting to eat its own vomit. Eating vomit is in its nature. At the end of his discourse regarding false prophets, Peter uses the example of the pig that returns to wallow in the mud. It likes the mud. The mud is comfortable to the pig. The pig doesn't understand or care about cleanliness.

Wallowing in mud is in its nature.

To illustrate the difference between man's natures, Jesus uses the illustration of trees. In Matthew chapter 7 Jesus says that a good tree is incapable of producing bad fruit and a bad tree is incapable of producing good fruit. An apple tree, for example, is a good tree. An apple tree produces apples. It is incapable of producing any other type of fruit. That doesn't mean there won't be an occasional worm eaten apple hanging on the tree or that the fruit will not rot. But the apple tree will never accidentally produce a thistle. Conversely, the only type of tree that is capable of producing an apple is an apple tree.

Once the nature of something is known, what can be expected of it is also known. To carry the illustration of the apple tree a little further, there are differences between the natures of various apple trees. For example, an apple tree that bears Golden Delicious apples cannot one year accidentally produce Granny Smith apples.

Man is born with a sinful nature. The fruit of that nature is described in Galatians 5:19-21. It is highly improbable that any one person would commit all of the 17 things that Paul lists there, but each item on the list is widely practiced, sometimes with passion or celebration. Man is powerless to change the nature with which he was born.

The only way for a sinful nature to change is if God changes it. Jesus called it a new birth. It involves the creative power of God, which is why scripture refers to those whose nature has been changed by God as new creations. The source of the new nature is God Himself. From God it extends to His new creations through Jesus. Jesus describes His relationship with the disciples as He Himself being the vine and His disciples being the branches. Christians are never described in the New Testament as creating the fruit of God's nature, but in obedience, bearing that fruit.

The fruit of God's nature is also described in Galatians 5. The nine aspects of that fruit flow from the Spirit of God through those who have been recreated in their own spirit and are undergoing a process of change through their entire being.

Even after people become Christians through a divine act of regeneration, however, they still struggle with the habits of the nature with which they were born. Paul dedicates the 7th and 8th chapters of Romans to the struggle between God's new nature operating through a Christian and what some have called "the old man of the flesh."

Old habits die hard. Old beliefs are hard to unlearn. Faith is scary.

Paul gives a hint of his own personal struggle in the 12th chapter of his second letter to Corinth. He speaks of a demon constantly mistreating him and compared the experience to having a wooden splinter in his side. He says he prayed several times for God to intervene. God's answer was "No." Instead he was given the mercy and strength to endure. Paul never specifically identifies what he was struggling with, perhaps out of his own shame or possibly to avoid glorifying or excusing for someone else whatever it was.

To say that homosexuals are born that way is neither breaking news nor should it be used as an excuse to justify abominable behavior. To use that excuse for sinful behavior is tantamount to Adam's response when God confronted him about eating the forbidden fruit. Adam basically said, "God, it's your fault. Everything was fine until you sent me that woman." Paul never justified the thorn in his side. He struggled against it, comforted and strengthened by the grace of God.

In another context it's easy to see how clearly wrong a propensity toward sexual perversion is, even though a person was born that way. The Diagnostic and Statistical Manual of Mental Disorders or DSM, classifies pedophilia as a mental disorder. The DSM is the psychiatrist's handbook.

Pedophiles are considered to be born with that nature, and it is a part of their sickness. Presently, there is no cure for pedophilia. Based on those two premises, it is legal in many states to indefinitely incarcerate a sex offender diagnosed as a pedophile. That means civil incarceration after they have completed their criminal incarceration in prison. Both premises are in harmony with the Biblical view of man's unregenerate nature. Very few would argue today that pedophiles should be left alone to fulfill their urges because they were born that way, and they are just being who they are. Very few would argue for pedophile rights and castigate the church for calling them sinners and failing to show real love.

It hasn't been that long ago since earlier versions of the DSM classified homosexuality as a mental disorder and the law and public opinion dealt with it in the same way that they presently handle pedophilia.

I Love My Son

A great deal of confusion is created in the church and in the mind of Christians when love is thrown into the equation. The source of the confusion is within the understanding of what it means to love.

The most common understanding of the word today is the romantic feeling that one person has for another. More often than not, that is a selfish love with conditions and jealousy. The love that Jesus expects us to have for each other is sober and unselfish.

As any parent knows, children don't always want what's best for them. Parenting a child involves a mix of selfish and selfless love. Selfish love is possessive. It reasons, "I'm doing this for you because I want you and don't want to lose you." Selfless love is directive. It reasons, "I'm doing this for you because I know this is best for you." Accordingly, any parent that loves his children will make sure they have their coats on before going out to play in the snow, whether they want to wear them or not. Just as parents will teach their children to not lie or steal.

But what happens when selfish love and selfless love contradict? An example can be seen in the 22nd chapter of Genesis, the first time the word "love" occurs in the Bible. The bulk of the chapter deals with Abraham's test. When God told him to take Isaac to Moriah and offer him as a sacrifice, He describes Isaac as Abraham's only son whom he loves. Abraham had as much selfish love for Isaac as any parent has for his children. The test brought into conflict the love he had for Isaac and the love he had for God.

To understand what was going on with Abraham at Moriah, two things should be understood about God's tests. First of all, God never tests a man to discover how he's doing or if he meets a standard. God is omniscient and already knows. God allows testing to come in order for the man to know through experience that he is strong enough to meet the standard. God already knew how great a faith Abraham had and that his selfless love for God was stronger than his selfish love for his son. When the test was over, Abraham knew.

The second thing to understand is the type of testing God employs. There are two ways to test someone or something. One can test to standard or test to capacity. For example: a grade school teacher gives her students a math test over addition. They have been taught to add numbers up to 20. A test to standard may be composed of ten or fifteen questions containing addition problems of numbers up to twenty. A test to capacity would involve 50 or 100 problems with the first ten or fifteen problems involving numbers up to twenty and then getting increasingly more difficult with problems containing three and four digit numbers. The test to capacity is not designed for any student to complete, but to see how far and how accurately each student is able to perform. Some students may be discouraged by a test to capacity.

There are also two types of tests used for

inanimate objects. Suppose a company sells a table that is guaranteed to hold 300 pounds. To test the table to standard, 300 pounds is put on the table. If the table holds, it meets the standard. To test the table to capacity, 350 pounds is put on the table. If the table holds, another 50 pounds is put on the table. Weight is added until the table collapses. This type of test reveals the true strength of the table, but it also destroys the table.

God always tests to standard. The scripture promises that God never tests us beyond what we are capable of handling. When Abraham lifted the knife above Isaac, God stopped him. Abraham knew that God was truly the most important thing in his life. That did not diminish the love that he had for his son. It only put that love in perspective.

Another source of confusion is the result of the American culture that has crept into the day to day operations of the church. American Christians act like the scripture is one among many sources of truth. Right and wrong are subject to democratic vote, committee approval or the congregation gets to decide for themselves. So, one church votes to allow their clergy to practice homosexuality, another church votes to defrock clergy who acknowledge being homosexual. Subsequently, individuals decide what they want to believe and which church they want to be a part of. The confusion is amplified by the disunity and lack of accountability in the Christian church as a whole.

It's possible, even for ministers, with all the confusion surrounding the issue to make allowances in their heart for the sin of their son, brother, nephew, or even a close friend. After all, we are not to judge others but to show them Christian love.

Judgment is typically the end of the story in practice, a step taken as the last resort, while relationships endure. The only case where a Christian is to judge is when a person inside the church claims to be righteous while openly and blatantly ignoring or excusing himself for a very public sin. A judgmental attitude is never a good idea and not prone to do any good.

The New Testament cautions us to avoid judgment, but teaching, on the other hand, is included in the great commission. It is an element of discipleship. Shouldn't a man first disciple his own children? Colossians chapter three says to allow the Word of Christ to have such abundant influence that teaching and correction flow wisely. While it is impossible to force someone to learn, teaching can be a dispassionate way of revealing the truth.

In the fourth chapter of his second letter to Timothy, Paul warns him that days are coming in which men will pick their favorite teachers according to what they want to hear. He urges Timothy to be prepared to teach, encourage, and patiently rebuke men before they must stand before Jesus in judgment. If a Christian truly loves his son, brother, nephew, friend, or anyone else, he will know and share the truth with them while there is still time.

The truth is not a matter for public debate or vote. Jesus called the Holy Spirit the Spirit of truth and said that He will teach us the whole truth.

When Abraham was on top of that mountain in Moriah with his son tied up on an altar, he had a choice to make between the selfish love he had for his son and the selfless love to follow God's direction for his son. Not only did he learn that he loved God, but that God loved him and his son. By choosing God's direction, Abraham learned to trust Him even more. Isaac may not have comprehended at the time, but eventually he came to share the great faith of his father.

Too much emphasis is placed on feelings when deciding between right and wrong. Decades ago, the concept slipped into the American consciousness by means of popular literature and music that declared, for example, that adulterous affairs couldn't possibly be wrong since they felt so right. Now feelings are used as the basis to justify homosexuality. However, something isn't right just because it feels right. Feelings are the most deceptive and unreliable part of the human existence. Forgiveness is always right, for instance, though it naturally doesn't feel good.

God never asks parents to stop loving their son, but He expects the parents to truthfully reflect His words and character. God is love and has nothing but love toward every man, even those that reject Him. But the sin is still immoral even if the whole world took a poll and decided unanimously otherwise.

Scripture is often deep and sometimes difficult to understand, but it is never the source of confusion.

Slavery and Freedom

Paul says in Romans chapter 6 that the person who volunteers to be a slave is still in reality a slave of the one he obeys. He says this in the middle of a long discussion about man's nature and legal standing before God. In that chapter, he looks at man's condition in terms of slavery and freedom.

Christians voluntarily commit themselves to Christ as their master. As a result, He works in their lives to free them from the power sin has over their thoughts, feelings, and will power. One could also say that Christians live for Christ. God's Spirit lives within them and, from the day of their new birth, He begins to whittle away the influence of sin in their lives. As long as they strive to obey Jesus, they will do the right thing in the eyes of God.

The people who do not know Jesus don't even realize when they displease God. Sin has no meaning for them, thus the necessity of the law. Paul would say such people are free in regards to God since He is not a part of their life at all. Atheists speak truthfully when they assert that they are free from guilty feelings.

People who do not know Jesus are enslaved instead by their own desires, bedeviled by problems they don't understand and without hope of any deep peace or joy. The major disadvantage escapes them while they try to live their lives in the condition of being spiritually dead. Spiritual life is not something that can be pretended with any greater success than a corpse can have pretending to be alive physically.

Can a homosexual be a Christian? Absolutely yes. Any person who realizes their offense to God, who realizes that God does not hate them but wants to perfect them, who realizes that God wants to fill their life with joy and good things, can become a Christian. The first step in becoming a Christian is surrender to God. And as every Christian knows, God, through His Spirit, begins working to change those things which are incompatible with His light. He begins the long process of cleaning house, so to speak. When God works with the homosexual, as well as any other sinner, there is no, "Poof! Now you're perfect."

The housecleaning is a lifelong process that is occasionally interrupted by the reluctant Christian who tells God, "Don't go into that closet." That request might be motivated by fear, but any sin can lead to slavery, and the contents of the off limits room is more likely a reliable sign that slavery is present there. As the Spirit gently works with individuals to open their eyes to the consequences of a particular servitude, and as their trust in Him grows, the door is likely to open. Some doors take longer to open than others though.

The point Paul makes in Romans 6 is that we choose our masters, and our choices have consequences. The devil is the master of confusion and deception, but individuals choose between God and their own way. Isaiah makes it clear in several passages that men are incapable of going God's way without His help, in case anyone thinks he can figure out how to live a God pleasing life on his own. Choosing our own way necessitates serving our own impulses and fighting our own struggles. Choosing to surrender to Christ obliges us to put our struggles in His hands and simply obey Him. The conflict between right and wrong is still there, but the pressure is off since the victory is already certain.

John also makes clear the fact that Christians are not sinless. He uses the analogy of walking in the light of God versus walking in the darkness of this world. Sin is incompatible with the nature of a Christian. Therefore, when a Christian sins, it bothers him. John goes so far as to say that if sin is not bothersome to someone, he might not be a Christian at all. Of course, all of this is taking place on the inside. It is the war between the conscience and the mind that Paul described in Romans chapter seven. Only the person involved in the battle knows it's going on.

Homosexuals in the Bible

First of all, there is not a single individual in the Bible who is clearly identified as a homosexual. Some have taken this absence to infer that the scripture gives tacit approval to the practice. Others find homosexuals hiding behind every tree in the Bible.

Homosexual rights is a contemporary cause taken up by many, some within various Christian denominations. But humans have a tendency to embrace a cause without fully understanding it and then blindly pursuing it at all costs, ignoring any truths which might interfere. This may lead them into trouble when the basic premise of the cause sounds good or righteous. From the very beginning, Eve, in her gullibility, thought she was doing a good thing when she ate the forbidden fruit. Adam, by the way, is not on record for putting up any fuss when she handed him the forbidden fruit.

Such was the case with Paul at the beginning of the book of Acts. He reasoned that since Jesus was executed as a criminal and His followers were outlawed by the Jewish authorities, he was undertaking a righteous cause in bringing the Christians to justice. Any indication to the contrary was just meaningless noise to him until Jesus miraculously intervened and brought Paul to his knees. It was only then that he was willing to examine all the evidence.

Such was the case with the temperance movement within the United States. Scripture is not silent on the prudent use of alcohol or lacking admonitions against drunkenness. But well-meaning Christians who had observed and possibly been the victims of the destructive power of alcohol reasoned that all alcohol was bad for everyone and worked within the political system to have it outlawed. They completely ignored passages of scripture such as Paul's advice to Timothy to stop drinking water exclusively since a little wine (*oinos*) would be good for his stomach and would improve his health. But even more perversely, some went so far as to say that the word translated as "wine" should really be translated as "new wine" which really meant grape juice. They either ignored or reinterpreted passages such as the one in Ephesians where Paul commanded them to refrain from drinking so much wine (*oinos*) as to get drunk. Yet, the word for "new wine" used in scripture exclusively in Acts 2 is not *oinos*, but *gleukos*.

A person's culture can be a significant barrier to understanding scripture. Many Americans tend to see everything from a myopic, present day, American point of view. For example, a group of about 300 students from a prominent Christian university in the south went on a mission trip to Southeast Asia shortly after the war in Vietnam. The biggest shock they encountered was not the strange dress or food, but finding believing Christians and established churches. It never occurred to them that a viable, spirited church existed outside of the United States. The culture of the Bible is foreign to the culture of 21st century America. To put scripture in context may also require knowing something about the culture of the area at the time it was written.

An example of using one's own culture to interpret others' actions could be found in Germany back when there were hundreds of thousands of American soldiers there. Young GI's were perplexed when they saw women walking down the street holding hands and jumped to the conclusion that they were lesbians. It was fairly common in Germany to see friends, especially younger people, walking along holding hands regardless of their gender. There was no sexual relationship implied by their action. That expression of friendship was normal and a part of their culture. Friends and even acquaintances in many countries greet each other or say goodbye with a kiss on the cheek. The peck on the cheek has nothing to do with a sexual relationship; it is a part of their culture.

A similar custom, greeting with a hug, is slowly creeping into the US through the southwest border.

Several characters in the Bible have been accused of being openly homosexual. Let us examine the most prominent of these in light of the context of the passages sighted and in view of the culture of their setting and time.

In the 18th chapter of 1st Samuel, David, the future king of Israel, and Jonathan, the son of Saul, are described as becoming soul mates. The first verse literally says they were bound together in their psyche. Then in the first chapter of 2nd Samuel, David mourns the death of his close friend Jonathan and says the love they shared was better than the love of women. These passages of scripture are very popular among proponents of homosexuality, even in some churches.

A soul mate is a wonderful thing to have. A soul mate would be a person's very best and probably life-long friend. Soul mates do not have to be married. In today's world they may not even live within commuting distance of each other. To be sure, the best marriages are between soul mates, but many people are not that fortunate. Best friends are very often of the same sex, but that in no way implies that sexuality is involved in the friendship. There are countless examples of deep friendships throughout western culture that were completely platonic.

David's confession at the beginning of 2nd Samuel attests to his deep friendship with Jonathan. He didn't say or even imply that their sex was better than natural sex. The word "love" means quite a bit more than sex. David said that their friendship was better than sex; deeper than sex; more meaningful than sex. Sex is gratifying, to be sure, but temporary. The close, harmonious relationship between two souls is more transcendent. As nearly half of all people who get married in America can affirm, sex won't get a relationship through the tough times. Souls that are joined together, however, can weather incredible hardship.

David was not a perfect man, but his heart was commended by God. On one occasion, he spotted a beautiful woman bathing on a rooftop. He was so sexually attracted to her that he arranged to have her husband killed in battle so he could marry her. In this instance he was a conniving, powerfully wicked king who managed to work out all the details to avoid perceptibly breaking God's law. But God immediately dispatched a prophet to David to let him know that he was being held accountable for adultery, covetousness, and murder, all that had transpired in his heart.

It is hardly likely that David could carry on a homosexual affair, something God hated, and not be reproved by Him. If the love David had in his heart for Jonathan had been of a sexual nature, he would have certainly been rebuked and not praised for it.

While there are certain aspects of the law that were clarified, such as the law about the

Sabbath, and some that were changed, such as certain dietary restrictions, the New Testament is clear that God still hates homosexual behavior.

Jesus did not negate the command to honor the Sabbath. He did, nonetheless, clarify on several occasions for the religious leaders of His day what it means to honor the Sabbath. The additions and changes they had made to the law over time through their tradition were not scriptural and had in fact steered God's people off course and corrupted their understanding of the Sabbath. One of Satan's commonly used deceptive tricks is adding to God's words. Perhaps that is why adding to the prophecy of The Revelation is punished as severely as detracting from it.

Jesus, Luke, and Paul all discuss changes in the dietary laws in the New Testament. Jesus says in Mark 7 that a person's thoughts and desires are the source of corruption, not what they eat. In Acts 10, Luke describes the vision Peter had before he went to minister to a gentile at Joppa wherein God tells him that He has cleansed the food he saw which was formerly unclean. Paul devotes most of Romans 14 to teach that Christians must let their conscience dictate what is permissible to eat and accordingly to refrain from judging others for what they eat.

While we gain new insight into the law regarding the Sabbath and the abomination of eating unclean food, there is no place in the New Testament where homosexual behavior is mentioned except in the light of judgment. There is not even a hint that the law forbidding homosexual behavior has changed or has been reinterpreted.

Yet, some proponents of homosexuality go so far as to suggest that Jesus and John, the disciple that Jesus loved, were in a homosexual affair. They point to passages such as where John leans on Jesus' breast during the last supper as evidence. This is a preposterous suggestion on many levels.

First of all, as discussed already, love doesn't equal sex. In particular, the Greek word for erotic love, *eros*, is not used in the Bible a single time. When the gospel of John refers to the disciple that Jesus loved, the words *agapao* and *phileo* are used. *Agapao* is a self-sacrificing love like a mother would have for her children or like the love God has for His people. *Phileo* is brotherly love or close friendship. It is where the city of brotherly love, Philadelphia, gets its name. It is also where the word "philosophy" comes from (*phileo* = love + *Sophia* = wisdom) and "philanthropy" (*phileo* = love + *anthropos* = man). No one has a problem in distinguishing between the meanings of the words "homosexual" and "philanthropist" because *phileo* does not imply sex.

On an even deeper level, the apostle John was Jesus' first cousin, the son of his mother's sister. It is widely believed that John may have been as young as 15 and Jesus was believed to have been in his thirties by the time of the last supper. To suggest that Jesus had a homosexual affair with John would also imply that Jesus was an incestuous pedophile. It is difficult to believe that any Christian, no matter how corrupted, could hold such a view of Jesus.

The method of taking a verse or part of a verse from the Bible to prove something is known as proof-texting. While there are occasions where a single verse does in fact sum up the passage from which it is taken, proof-texting can be dangerous because the user confidently asserts what the verse literally says, but what the verse in context may not be saying.

For example, 1st Corinthians 2:9 is used to substantiate that no one has any idea what heaven is like. The verse does indeed state that no one has ever seen, nothing has ever been heard, and no one can even imagine what God has prepared for them that love Him. Nevertheless, the following verse says that God's Spirit has revealed those things to His people.

In another example, the first few words of Romans 8:28, which say that everything works together for good, are often quoted. The rest of the verse limits that statement to the benefit of those who are chosen by God and who love Him. While God does indeed work everything for the benefit of all men, He will not intervene and force His will upon those who willfully reject Him for the deceiver who is out to destroy them.

It shouldn't come as a surprise that those who suggest homosexuality is approved in the Bible also use proof-texting. An often used example is Ezekiel 16:49. Already discussed in detail earlier, the verse says that the sin of Sodom was that in her arrogance she did nothing to sustain or support the poor and the downcast, even though she had plenty of food and free time. This verse is taken out of context to imply that homosexuality had nothing to do with God's anger or Sodom's destruction. It was the city's mistreatment of the poor. It was their failure to love, not their "love" that brought about God's anger. A Christian might well be confused if that's all that was said. But the next verse goes on to say that the people of Sodom became haughty and committed abomination, and for that reason God removed them. Remember, all this happened before the law spelled out that homosexual acts are an abomination to God.

There are many examples where proof-texting is used to support the false idea that the Bible condones homosexual practice. For illustration, one more example will be considered. In 1st Kings chapter 20, verses 32 and 33, Ahab, the king of Israel, refers to Ben-Hadad as his brother and invites him into his chariot. This short clip of scripture is used by proponents of homosexual behavior as one of many clips to illustrate that homosexuality was common and not frowned upon in the Bible.

To put the clip in context, it is necessary to read from the first verse of the chapter. Ben-Hadad was the king of Syria and an enemy of Israel long before Ahab became its king. One day he decided to go to war against Israel with the intention of confiscating all of their valuable possessions, including their wives and children. He along with his allies attacked Israel several times, and God miraculously defeated him each time though his armies vastly outnumbered Israel's army. There is no indication in scripture that the two kings had ever met before Ben-Hadad attacked. By the point in the chapter where the clip is taken, Ben-Hadad was afraid for his life and had approached Ahab on the battlefield to beg for mercy. Contrary to what God had directed, Ahab made a land deal with Ben-Hadad and let him go. Once the context is understood, it is beyond bizarre to suggest that the passage implies that Ahab had a spontaneous homosexual tryst with Ben-Hadad.

One of the strongest rebukes delivered to any single person in the Bible was conveyed to Ahab by Elijah. He is condemned for murder, theft, following the wicked advice of his wife Jezebel, and the abomination of practicing idolatry. Elijah would certainly have included the abomination of having sex with another man if it were true. Interesting to note, Ahab repented and was spared the calamity prophesied against him.

Distortion of the Picture

Throughout the Bible, God has painted pictures of His character and the way He operates. The story of Noah, for instance, teaches that there is a limit to how far God will allow man to stray before he draws the line. It also paints a picture of God's chosen people, safely tucked inside the ark while the earth experiences major calamity outside. It further illustrates that God had a plan and shared with His servant as much as he needed to know.

The law of God is a vast and intricate self-portrait. When God gave Moses the law, He stressed the point that he should be attentive to carry out and fulfill the smallest details. Paul said in Romans that the law was a tutor for

God's people to prepare them for Christ. Through the law, God was painting a picture of His plan for salvation along with other lessons. The smallest facets of the picture were used to foreshadow and illustrate what would come to pass thousands of years later.

Pictures such as Passover illustrated Jesus on the cross. From the unblemished lamb to the placement of the blood, any follower of God at the time of Christ should have been able to see what was happening. Let's take the placement of the blood. Crucifixion was the common form of capital punishment when Jesus was sentenced to death. Countless criminals had been crucified with blood at the sides and bottom of the crosses. In the instructions for Passover, God told Moses to place the lamb's blood on the lintel, or top piece of the door. Unlike other criminals who were crucified, Jesus was bleeding from His head where the crown of thorns had been thrust. The placement of the blood was one of numerous details involved in Passover that God told Moses to be careful to prepare exactly as instructed. God was painting a picture.

The tabernacle is another example of a detailed picture God painted through the law. The outer walls of the tabernacle were alternating colors: red for man, blue for God, and purple for God and man coming together, a foreshadowing of Christ, the intermediary. Everything about the tabernacle was related to man and God coming together. The details, however, painted a picture of Jesus. Inside the holy place of the tabernacle was bread on the altar of showbread, prayer through the altar of incense, and light on the menorah. During His ministry, Jesus told people that He was the bread of life and the true bread which came down out of heaven. He also said that He was the light of the world and that He was the only way to God.

When Jesus died, the tabernacle revealed other truths through carefully described details. The furnishings of the tabernacle were placed in the shape of a cross. Paul said that Jesus is the mercy seat, the cover of the Ark of the Covenant inside the most holy place in the tabernacle, upon which the blood of the annual offering for atonement was placed. Another aspect of the tabernacle picture was the instruction that only the high priest could enter the most holy room, and he could only enter once a year. A heavy curtain separated the most holy place from the rest of the tabernacle. When Jesus died, the separating curtain hanging in the temple in Jerusalem tore in half from top to bottom. Was it just a coincidence that the curtain gave way at that particular time, or was God using the intricate picture He had painted to show that Jesus was bringing His own blood before God and opening the way for anyone who would follow to come directly into God's presence?

Marriage is another remarkable picture that God uses to teach His people about Himself. The picture begins with the creation of Adam and Eve. Genesis points out that God created all the animals after He created Adam but before He created Eve. Each one was brought to Adam for companionship and to help him. Adam may have liked many of the animals, but none were suitable as his helper and companion. God, of course, knew this from the start. But by holding off on Eve's creation, God was teaching Adam that she was special. She could do for him what no animal could do. She could relate to him in ways no animal could.

God didn't need to perform the first surgery to collect one of Adam's ribs as a blueprint for Eve. But by making her that way God made it clear to Adam that she was a part of him. She wasn't merely an excellent copy. She wasn't another animal. As Adam said when he saw her, "My bone is her bone and my flesh is her flesh."

On the occasion referred to earlier, recorded in Matthew chapter 19, Jesus was confronted by the Pharisees on the issue of divorce. They posed their question to Him because one of the theological arguments that concerned them was the standard by which divorce was permissible. The Pharisees wanted to know where Jesus stood on the issue. In His answer, Jesus referred to the creation of Eve, noting that God had created man as male and female, and God said, "For this reason." Jesus was using the picture to explain to the Pharisees the origin and permanence of marriage.

Marriage between a man and a woman is a natural consequence of creation. When God created Adam's helper, it was not another male. Eve was not Adam number two. Eve was different because God was painting a picture through which He would teach man something about Himself. Perhaps the first and most important lesson to learn is that man is not God.

Paul sheds more light on the picture in the

5th chapter of Ephesians where he shows that a godly marriage is an accurate depiction of the relationship between Christ and the church. In several passages in the New Testament he describes the church as the body of Christ, but in Ephesians 5:30 he alludes to the creation of Eve and says that our flesh is His flesh and our bones are His bones.

When Paul gives the instruction to the wife in verse 22 to submit to her husband the same way she submits to the Lord, he is not belittling the wife. In the next verse, he explains that God has placed the wife under the husband's authority in the same way the church is under Christ's authority. Instead of being another husband, she has her own responsibilities as the wife, responsibilities she is particularly suited to by means of her unique creation, even as the church is not Christ but has tremendous responsibility to carry out its mission under His authority. This position becomes critical when in verse 25 he commands the husband to love his wife in the same way that Christ loves the church.

A position of authority is in reality a position of responsibility; the greater the authority, the greater the responsibility. God is responsible for everything because He is the supreme authority.

Paul lays out in the letter to the Ephesians several responsibilities for the husband. First, the husband is required to love his wife sacrificially. The word used here for love is *agapao* which is self-sacrificing love, and it is used in the active voice, imperative mood. He is also to help her become a better Christian by being a minister of the Word of God to her. He is to nurture her and be tender toward her. The word used in 5:29 translated most often as cherish literally means to keep her warm.

Before Paul concludes his teaching on marriage by restating his instructions to the wife and husband, he quotes the passage in Genesis 3 referring to the creation of Eve, a passage that the New Testament refers to four times. By quoting the passage of Eve's creation in this context, Paul is affirming the picture God created when He instituted marriage through the creation of Adam and Eve.

Homosexual marriage distorts the picture of marriage that God painted in scripture. By distorting that picture, it also sends a confusing message about the relationship between Christ and the church, or on a larger scale, between God and mankind. Whether both partners are male or both partners are female makes no difference. In a homosexual marriage both partners have equal claim to the role of husband and wife.

In essence, homosexual marriage paints a completely different picture than the one God intended. It paints the picture of man's equality with God. The church can decide whether or not to follow Christ, because as His equal, the church has equal authority. The picture painted by homosexual marriage harkens back to the lie the serpent fed Eve in the Garden of Eden. "There is no harm in eating this fruit. God is only giving this instruction because He is afraid that you will become His equal." Today the serpent has a new lie. "There is no harm in same sex marriage. Let them be happy, and mind your own business."

It shouldn't surprise anyone that a godless person is completely lost concerning God and what He wants. But a Christian should know better.

A popular argument to discount the teaching of scripture on homosexual issues is that God's people weren't ready in New Testament times for the progression of His permissiveness. They reasoned that since God changed the laws on diet and relaxed the law of the Sabbath, it is sensible to conclude that He would accept homosexuality today.

Explaining that God now accepts homosexuality based on those perceived changes is a mistake for several reasons. First of all, man did not approach God as a result of his own cravings to petition for the changes. The changes were initiated by Jesus. Jesus also said that the law was perfect and eternal. The picture painted by the Sabbath has not changed. God still wants us to know that He is able to take care of us in any circumstance.

The dietary laws were transformed, but they are still a good idea. For example, even with today's technology, pork is one of the most harmful foods one can eat. An occasional pork chop or pork roast is delicious. But a diet consisting predominantly of pork can be disastrous health wise. One clue should be the fact that pork must undergo a curing process before it is fit for consumption.

There is a difference between the perfect will of God and the accommodating or permissive will of God. For example, God permitted divorce, but He never intended it. The husband and wife who work through their issues for the sake of Christ will reap rewards down the road. But those things that God accepts even reluctantly are revealed in scripture. Certain things that cannot and will not change are also made clear in the Bible.

Not the Super Sin

There is no doubt that homosexual behavior is a sin, but it is not the unforgivable sin. And while an unrepentant homosexual may be on the road to committing the unforgivable sin, they are no more on the road than anyone who is unrepentant of any sin. The key to God's forgiveness is repentance and obedience to His leading. Paul teaches in his letter to the Romans that man is drawn to repentance by God's goodness.

Christians who struggle with homosexual urges are in the same boat as Christians who struggle with alcohol or food or any other temptation. Unfortunately, religious people have a tendency to set themselves up as some sort of self-appointed spiritual police. Even in Jesus day, the devout Jews were quick to point out other people's faults. In Matthew chapter 7 Jesus asked them why. Specifically, He asked them why they ignored the beam in their own eye to point out the twig in their brother's eye. Nearly every time the subjects of condemnation or forgiveness came up in the gospel narrative, Jesus pointed out another human tendency. We tend to ignore or diminish our own struggles and shortcomings.

The only sexual sin included in the Ten

Commandments is the sin of adultery. But when a woman who was caught in the very act of adultery was brought to Jesus for sentencing, He forgave her and told her to refrain from future sin. He did not by any means imply that she had not sinned. He knew that she had sinned. She knew that she had sinned. He did point out, however, that her accusers were no more free from sin than she was.

It's interesting to note that the worship of a fertility goddess was common throughout the ancient near east, and God's people were constantly being drawn away to her altars. References to Asherah, the Queen of Heaven, pillars or altars on the high places or mountains, all refer to worship of what the Canaanites understood to be the spouse of Baal, their chief god. Throughout the period of the kings of Israel and Judah, each monarch was judged by, among other things, how he dealt with this special form of idolatry. Wicked kings such as Ahab promoted and participated in the cult. Good kings such as Josiah tore down the altars on the high places.

Sexual sins are easy targets and rallying points for criticism because they are obvious. The detractors feign their own virtue. But even Jesus refused the moniker "good" saying that God alone is good. If Jesus, the Son of God, refused to assert His own piety, how can any of His followers dare assume the position of judge?

Sin behaves the same way no matter what it is. The essence of sin is meeting a legitimate need in an illegitimate way or trying to be someone else. Needs can foster wants and temptation. The Christian who does not recognize temptation has already lost the battle. David began the 23rd Psalm with a declaration against temptation. He realized that he had a choice of masters in life. On one hand he could be led by his own wants and needs, letting his desires take him wherever. On the other hand he could be led by the Lord. He announced that the Lord was his shepherd, not his own desires. Wants and needs must be evaluated in the light of God's direction. If God has said, "No" or, "Not now", there is always a good reason. The timing in meeting a need is often as important as meeting the need itself. To affirm that homosexual behavior is a sin is not to deny that a legitimate need underlies the temptation. But sin usually takes the quick and easy solution.

"There is nothing that keeps wicked men at any one moment out of hell, but the mere pleasure of God."

- Jonathan Edwards

WHAT'S NEXT

Worse than Your Sisters

The 16th chapter of Ezekiel begins with the words, "Son of man, cause Jerusalem to know her abominations." An extensive prophesy against the holy city fills the lengthy chapter. The sin of Sodom is mentioned because God is accusing Jerusalem of being worse than Sodom. The chapter relates God's goodness to the city when she was young and struggling to survive when all the nations around her hated her. It recounts the blessings and riches God poured into her and how she became the envy of the world at the time.

But Jerusalem, and Judah by extension, grew to take God for granted and, just like Lucifer, turned from following and worshipping Him to worshipping itself. Instead of thanking God for His blessing, they convinced themselves that they alone were responsible for their wealth and beauty. By the time Ezekiel was writing, idolatry was commonplace. The people whom God had chosen, blessed, and set apart were worshipping the gods of neighbor nations as their own.

In addition to idolatry they committed further abomination with the sacrifice of their children. They believed that some of the false deities they worshipped demanded human sacrifice so they offered their own children. But God told them their children belonged to Him, and He condemned them for the heartless practice.

The book of Ezekiel begins with a final warning to Judah, all that's left of God's people. By the 16th chapter, God let His people know that the neighboring countries all despised them due to their wickedness. He also let them know that He was about to turn them over to their enemies. No more miraculous rescues. He was removing the hedge of protection. God promised them in that chapter that His favor would be with anyone who confronted them. Ezekiel finished writing his prophecies counting the years as a prisoner of Nebuchadnezzar in Babylon.

The United States shows all the signs of rebellion and wickedness that Judah showed just prior to her judgment and exile. The decay in America has surpassed that of God's people at their worst. Not only do we worship every god brought to our land from every nook of the world, under the guise of fairness, we officially deny God's presence at all. People set themselves up as gods. The American god who we are all called by our government to serve, the U.S. Constitution, is the source of our rights.

America has made life, liberty, and the pursuit of happiness a god and happily sacrifices its children thereto. Neighbors on every side despise America for its arrogance and wickedness. She has become a laughing stock the world over, ripe for the judgment of God, just as His people were at the time of Ezekiel and Jeremiah.

It's My Body

Deriving from the rights to life, liberty, and the pursuit of happiness is the idea that Americans are free to do whatever they want as long as it doesn't infringe on someone else's right to life, liberty and their pursuit of happiness. If an American wants to abuse his own body or destroy his own property he is free to do so as long as it doesn't hurt anyone else.

God says that children are His gift and His blessing to us. Americans agree as long as it's convenient. When it's inconvenient, an unborn child becomes nothing more than superfluous tissue that is not really alive yet.

So in the name of a woman's right to make decisions concerning her own body and for her own convenience, the child is murdered. The doctors who perform the murder are fully aware of the fact that an embryo, no matter how young, can be placed in another woman's womb and grow. That is so because the child has its own life apart from the callous incubator that wants to kill it.

In England, many years ago, a married couple who had tried to have children for nearly a decade discovered that the wife's fallopian tubes were blocked. Through advances in modern medicine, their daughter, Louise Brown, was conceived in a petri dish. Instead of throwing her in the garbage as a nearly invisible speck of useless tissue, the doctors took care of her and placed her in her mother's womb. Today Louise is married with children of her own.

But perversion is a progression. The same rights that a woman has over her own body eventually translate to all people having rights over their own bodies. There are already those who want the right to eat, drink, smoke, or inject whatever they want into their own bodies. Already, a majority of states have made smoking and eating marijuana legal for medical reasons, and the push is on to legalize it for any reason. Will the legalization of opiates be next? After all, there is a sizable population in the country living in unbearable pain. Shouldn't they have the right to use the all drugs they want for medical reasons? It's their body.

An extension of the "it's my body" rationale is the concept of consenting adults. Proponents of homosexual behavior include this rationale as an argument for accepting the practice. After all, if two men want to pursue happiness by having sex, then they should be free to do so. As long they both consent, it's their bodies. No one else is affected and therefore should not be concerned. They reject John Donne's postulate that, "No man is an island entire of itself. Every man is a piece of the continent, a part of the main."

Constitutionally Protected Class of People

Proponents of homosexual behavior draw similarities between the plight of homosexuals fighting for their constitutional rights and American slaves of the 19th century. A major source of confusion can be laid at the feet of Christian churches of the day located in the Old South which misused scripture to justify the practice. The Bible makes no distinction regarding race for any reason.

As far as the issue of slavery in America goes, the 13th amendment to the constitution which became law in 1865 does not mention slaves, per se. It prohibits the practice of forcing someone to work against their will except as punishment in the case of a duly convicted criminal.

Several amendments have been made to the constitution to address what amounts to discrimination. In particular, amendments address discrimination based on sex, race, and age in certain matters. For example, the 15th amendment guarantees the right to vote for Americans of all races.

Shifty lawyers and judges equate those who practice homosexuality to the classes of people protected by the constitution. The argument hinges on the fact that homosexuals are born that way and have no choice in the matter. There is no question that some men are born with homosexual desires. Everyone is born with a perverted, sinful nature. There is a difference, however, between those who practice homosexuality and the classes of people protected by the constitution.

A people cannot change their race any more than they can change their age. When a person turns 18 in America, for example, their right to vote is constitutionally protected by the 26th amendment. If they are only one week away from turning 18, they have no constitutionally protected right to vote. They cannot decide to be 18 because they desperately want to vote. In one week's time they will become a member of that class of constitutionally protected people. At that point, they cannot choose to be excluded from the class. Parenthetically, there is no moral basis for determining the correct voting age.

A person who practices homosexuality can choose whether or not to do so. Just as any person can choose to be celibate, as many men and women have done through the ages. There are no constraining factors that force a person to practice homosexuality. Those who practice homosexuality do so by choice.

If five of the justices of the Supreme Court decide that those who practice homosexuality are a constitutionally protected class of people, there is another group waiting in the wings. They must go through a similar process to gain acceptance and legal protection. Some of them have already begun the course.

In western civilization, homosexual behavior was initially condemned by the Bible, and the earliest offenders were punished or rehabilitated by the church. By the 16th century, civil courts began to take over prosecuting crimes and followed, for the most part, the church's lead. By the 19th century, homosexuality was wrested from the courts by the medical field of psychiatry. Prominent psychiatrists argued about the causes, but most agreed it was some form of sexual abnormality. The main consequence of the behavior moving out of the legal system and into the field of psychology was its decriminalization.

Homosexuality was classified as a mental disorder in the original Diagnostic and Statistical Manual of Mental Disorders in 1952. By the mid 60's, the gay rights movement in America had gained considerable momentum and political power. By 1973, the American Psychiatric Association (APA) removed "Homosexuality" and replaced it with "Sexual Orientation Disturbance." That meant that homosexuality was only considered a mental illness if the individual was uncomfortable with it. The inevitable outcome of guaranteeing the personal right of pursuing happiness was having its effect. By the 1980's, there were members of the APA who were open and vocal concerning their own homosexual preferences. In 1987, homosexuality was completely removed from the DSM.

The APA removed the diagnosis based on years of intense study by many noted psychiatrists. The preponderance of evidence showed that those who practice homosexuality are in every other way normal. There was no reason to continue to diagnose homosexuality as a mental disorder.

The medical community then handed the issue of homosexual behavior back to the civil authority with the disclaimer that the behavior is normal. It is not within the purview of the medical community to say whether it is right or wrong.

The process was long but simple. The church mishandled the issue of homosexuality so the state stepped in and said, essentially, "We'll take it from here." The medical community stepped in to examine the issue and became the authority for the state. But the medical community rationalized that there's nothing really wrong or abnormal going on. They informed the state to reverse course. The problem comes when the state directs the church to reverse course.

There are some denominations that have reversed course. They take their direction from the state and public opinion. But the true church of God only takes direction from God and reverses course only on His direction.

The process is not limited to homosexual behavior. There are hundreds of paraphilias, many of which are still listed in the DSM such as zoophilia (sex with animals), pedophilia (sex with children), necrophilia (sex with dead bodies), voyeurism (sexual gratification from watching others), exhibitionism (sexual gratification by exposing one's self), masochism (sexual gratification through pain), and sadism (sexual gratification from inflicting pain) to name a few. In the same way as in the past, these medical diagnoses allow the state to lock away the deviants, either in hospitals or jails.

Just as with homosexuality, there are proponents of many of these practices pushing for them to become normalized and socially acceptable. The proponents of those deviant practices have a blueprint to follow in the standardization of homosexual behavior. As early as 1905, Sigmund Freud said that he knew homosexuals and pedophiles that were living normal lives in every other respect and questioned whether they could be considered abnormal. Evidence that the process is already underway can be seen in that when the APA declared that only those who had a problem with their homosexual preference were diagnosable, they also considered whether the same could be said of other paraphilias.

The latest version of the DSM classifies those acting on the urges of a paraphilia that victimize a non-consenting partner as mentally ill. Pedophilia is thus classified as a mental illness if the pedophile acts on his impulse since a child cannot legally consent. But what if the partner is consenting? There is already a movement to declassify pedophilia from the DSM. Hollywood has already produced movies where people have been emotionally and sympathetically exposed to the practice. At this stage, there are plenty of legal battles to fight and politicking to be done before the acronym LGBTQIAP becomes common and pedophiles become a constitutionally protected class of people.

In Leviticus chapter 18 where the law against homosexual behavior is spelled out, there are also prohibitions against adultery, incest, and bestiality. There is no mention of mental illness or defect concerning these sins. There is, though, an acknowledgement that people all over the region were doing these things without giving it a second thought.

When America was founded, adultery was a crime. The perpetrator could expect some sort of civil punishment as well as public humiliation and scorn. Today, adultery is so common it is almost expected. Sure, there is an occasional word spoken out in a church where the pastor is brave enough to offend some of his hearers, but most people pay no attention. So many pastors and evangelists have been caught in adultery that the message from God has become diluted.

Fifty years ago, homosexual behavior was a crime in most of the country. The perpetrator could expect some form of civil punishment as well as public humiliation and scorn. Today, the closet doors are open and public humiliation is directed against anyone who speaks a word against gay rights. Are incest and bestiality on the horizon of becoming socially acceptable in the United States? They are unless something changes because there are thousands more in other closets who reject the Word of God and want to practice their perversion openly with public approval. The US government and the Constitution as presently interpreted are their allies.

God Draws the Line

As much as things change, they also stay the same. Throughout history kingdoms and empires have come and gone, each group glorying in its accomplishments and proud of its status. God has blessed realms in former times, and He has destroyed wicked empires that have worn out His patience. How much longer will God put up with the evil in America?

The Bible talks about national sin in quite a few places, but perhaps no place is the discussion more focused than the book of Amos. Through the first few chapters, it is clear that God holds nations accountable for depravity just as he holds individuals accountable. When selfish leaders manipulate their people into following corruption, the whole land is judged.

The bulk of the book of Amos is directed at God's own people, the regions of Israel and Judah. Amos gives a lot of detail concerning specific injustices, a majority of which have to do with how the wealthy treat the poor of the land. In the last chapter, a warning is issued that God is watching the guilty nation and will bring devastation.

Here, in line with the common human perspective, the people were thinking, "It won't happen to us." But all sin brings judgment. Even without all the scriptural evidence, it follows logically that if God punishes the individual sinner, He also punishes the nation adrift in sin.

The likely question brought up when discussing God's judgment on a nation is, "What happens to the faithful?" Throughout scripture, when wholesale reckoning occurs, there are inevitably at least a few people who are faithful to God present in the mix. Historically, there are four ways that God's people have survived times of judgment.

Protected:
There are occasions in scripture where judgment came en masse but was not directed at

God's people. On some of these occasions, God protected His people while the destruction happened all around them.

One instance of this type of survival is described beginning in Genesis 6. The story of Noah is the fourth story in the Bible. Mankind had quickly turned to evil after creation. We are told that every thought man had and every intention of his heart was hurtful, and he was getting worse all the time. God said that He regretted making man and decided to destroy everything and start over.

But an interesting concept, central to the New Testament, is introduced in the eighth verse. Noah was given grace by God. There is no discussion of the reason he was extended grace beyond the short characterization in the following verse which describes Noah as reasonable, mature, and a follower of God.

God told Noah that He could not abide man's violence any longer, and He began to give him instructions on how to prepare for the destruction that was about to befall the world. When the flood waters came, Noah and all the animals that were entrusted to him were safely aboard the Ark.

Another example of God protecting His people in times of judgment can be found beginning in the eighth chapter of Exodus. Moses was sent to Pharaoh to demand that he release God's people. Pharaoh, unwilling to lose such a sizable free labor force was reluctant to agree to Moses' request. So God sent a series of plagues to destroy Egypt and change Pharaoh's mind.

In Exodus 8:21 God told Moses to warn

Pharaoh that swarms of gadflies would descend on all of Egypt if he didn't let His people go. The next verse, however, says that in order to prove He is God, the Lord would keep the pests out of the Land of Goshen in east Egypt where His people were living.

The same thing occurred in chapter 9 with the plague on the livestock of Egypt and the plague of the fire and hail. In all three cases, the passage points out that God protected His people from the judgment that fell on Egypt.

Evacuated:

One way God's people survive wholesale judgment that comes to their land is through evacuation. When God decided to destroy the cities of Sodom, Gomorrah, Admah, and Zeboiim, He spared the lives of Lot and his family by evacuating them from the city.

Lot's sons-in-law thought he was joking when Lot warned them to escape the impending destruction. Lot himself was in no hurry to leave so the angels who were sent to warn him had to physically drag him and his family away from the city.

God Relents:

There is much scriptural evidence that indicates God's judgment is always conditional. One of the most powerful and promising verses in the entire Bible is 2nd Chronicles 7:14, "If My people who are called by My name will humble themselves and pray and desire to be in My presence and turn away from their hurtful habits, then I will hear from heaven, forgive their sin, and heal their land."

On more than one occasion, God told Moses to separate himself from the people so He could destroy them and start over again with Moses. In Exodus 32, for example, when the people grew impatient with how long Moses had been gone and decided to make a golden calf and call it their god, God sensed their treacherous hearts and was ready to destroy them. Moses could have said nothing and become the father of a new nation of God's people.

Whether out of compassion for the people or for God, Moses intervened. He asked God to think about His reputation and what the Egyptians would think and say. He asked God to remember the promises He had made to Abraham, Isaac, and Israel. After Moses intervened, God changed His mind.

Ahab, the king of Israel, provides another example of God changing His mind about judgment. He wanted a vineyard close to the castle because it was convenient. The owner refused to give it away since it was the family's inheritance. Ahab's wife arranged to have the owner killed, and afterward, Ahab took possession of the vineyard. That act was the straw that broke the camel's back, so to speak. Ahab had already distinguished himself in God's eyes by the extent of his idolatrous life.

In the latter half of 1st Kings 21, Elijah pronounced a punishment and curse that God intended to bring against Ahab and his wife. He lays in to Ahab letting him know that he was the most wicked king that had ever sat on the throne.

After Ahab heard the judgment, he humbled himself before God and repented, even though he considered Elijah an enemy. In the last verse of the chapter God points out Ahab's repentance to Elijah and tells him that He changed His mind and will relent from punishing Ahab directly.

The book of Jonah has much to say about the compassion God's people should have for everyone, even those outside the assembly. God's willingness to change His mind concerning judgment is another significant point expressed in the short book.

God sent Jonah to Nineveh, one of the largest cities in the world at that time, with a message of judgment. Jonah famously ran away and was brought back by a large fish. Jonah knew the entire time what he was doing. He ran away because he wanted to see Nineveh destroyed. He hated the city and its inhabitants and didn't want to warn them of their impending doom. Jonah might have died in the whale had he not repented and told God that he would obey.

After Jonah adjusted his attitude, God instructed him again to go to Nineveh to warn the people there of the coming judgment. Jonah obeyed, alerting them that the devastation of the city was less than six weeks away. Remarkably, the people of Nineveh paid attention to the warning and reacted. The king of the city directed the entire population to cease their hurtful, selfish ways and plead for forgiveness from God.

When God saw that the people repented, He changed His mind and let them live. Jonah wasn't happy. In his own piety, he had hoped

God would destroy the wicked city. But God rebuked Jonah for his lack of compassion for more than 120,000 people who didn't know their right hand from their left.

Judgment:

Sometimes God's judgment is directed at His people. In such cases not all of God's people survive, and those that do survive must persevere. At other times, though the judgment is not specifically directed at God's people, they must go through the circumstances along with those at whom the punishment is aimed.

An example of the latter is found in Exodus 12. God warned Pharaoh of the severity of the tenth and final plague He would send. To His people in the land of Goshen, however, He spoke only of the preparations they needed to make in order to endure the plague. In the 12th verse He told them that He would move throughout the land of Egypt to strike down the first-born of every household. That included the land of Goshen on the eastern edge of Egypt where they were living. Only the houses He found that were marked on the front door with the blood of a lamb would be spared death. If any of God's people rebuffed Moses' words in their minds and subsequently failed to prepare, they lost their eldest child along with all the others in Egypt who did not know God.

The incident where God's people decided to make a golden calf and call it their god is both an example of God relenting, since He did not destroy them completely as He was initially inclined to do, and an example of God's judgment on His own people. When Moses came down from the mountain with the tablets containing the Ten Commandments and saw what the people were doing, he was disheartened and angry. God directed him to carry out His judgment on those who were guilty and on those who had decided not to follow the Lord. About three thousand died that day.

Another example can be found in the beginning chapters of 1st Samuel. Eli had been a priest and judge at the temple in the town of Shiloh for some time. Shiloh is significant as it was the first place God dwelled among his people, before the reign of David when Jerusalem still belonged to the Jebusites. By the time the Bible picks up his story in 1st Samuel, Eli had grown sons who had taken over the priestly duties. Eli's sons lived up to the bad reputation of some modern day preacher's kids. They disregarded God's laws for their own convenience and gain. Scripture specifically notes that they perverted the sacrifice and slept around with the women who served at the entrance of the temple.

God held Eli accountable for failing to correct the flippant behavior of his sons who were characterized by the prophet Samuel as good for nothing and strangers to God. The sign to Eli that God personally carried out the judgment against his sons was that both of them were killed on the same day. An additional blow to Eli that day was the report that the Philistines captured the Ark of the Covenant. After hearing all the bad news, Eli fell over and died. Neither Eli nor his sons survived the judgment against them.

In Luke 12 Jesus said that His servants would be held to a higher standard than those who do not know God. Peter echoed a truth found throughout scripture when he said that it is time for judgment to begin in the house of God.

One human weakness that Christians also suffer from is the tendency to put individuals on a pedestal. Analogous to hero worship or following the glamour of Hollywood, Christians tend to idolize popular preachers, evangelists, and those in lofty positions in the church. But the most influential and popular Christian leaders are merely human with all the weakness and temptation that being human involves. For those placed on pedestals, their chances of being judged grow in proportion to the extent they are deluded into believing that they are something more than they are.

God shows that He holds all of His people accountable from the lowest to the most honored from a human perspective. Another example of God's judgment of powerful, respected people can be found in the 15th chapter of 1st Samuel.

God had directed his chosen and anointed king, Saul, to punish the Amalekites for the way they treated His people during their flight from Egypt. Saul was explicitly ordered to completely annihilate them and destroy all of their possessions. He was to show no pity and leave no survivors, man or animal. Saul dutifully took his army and ambushed their king and battled against the people until they were all dead. But he took the king prisoner and the soldiers kept the livestock and any valuables they found.

Afterward, God told Samuel that he regretted

making Saul the king. God's judgment frequently follows His regret. Samuel was furious that Saul had turned away from God, and he prayed all night. When he met Saul the next day, Saul was cheerful and told him that he finished the task. Samuel ruined Saul's day with his reply. God expected Saul to carry out His instructions without exception. Saul's reasoning, that the animals could be used in sacrifices to God, was not an excuse for disobedience. Samuel lets Saul know that God prefers obedience over sacrifice.

Saul was fired that day from being king, and Samuel was instructed shortly after to anoint David as king in Saul's place. Samuel told Saul that David was a better man, not because he was stronger or anything to look at, but because of who he was on the inside. David is described later in scripture as a man after God's own heart.

Then again, even David disappointed God from time to time and became the target of God's judgment. On one such occasion, David had gone up to the roof about sunset to get some fresh air. While he was up there, he saw a woman taking a bath on a nearby rooftop. Now David was a married man and well acquainted with the law against adultery. But being a man, he worked out a scheme to get what he wanted. As the warrior king, he arranged for the woman's husband to be killed in battle. Then, as the consoling king, he married her.

David and Bathsheba had a baby, but God was unhappy with the whole affair. God pronounced judgment against David through the mouth of His prophet Nathan. The judgment against David was threefold. First, his descendants would always be involved in armed conflict. Second, all of his wives would be unfaithful to him. And last, his baby borne by Bathsheba would die.

Prior to pronouncing judgment, as is regularly done in scripture, God recounts to David all that He had done for him. He made him king, protected him when Saul tried to kill him, made him wealthy and would have given him much more if he had the need. In spite of all God had done, David acted in such a way that held God's commands, and ultimately God Himself, in contempt. David repented earnestly, and God forgave his sin. Nevertheless, he was still punished.

Aside from individual men of God being judged, there are many examples of God's judgment against His people as a nation. Leviticus 18, the chapter that prohibits homosexual behavior, incest, and bestiality, includes a warning. Should the people fall into the ways of the godless people they displaced, they too would be ejected from the land.

Ezekiel and Jeremiah were prophets during the time the nation of Judah was taken away into Babylonian captivity. Ezekiel 16, which has already been discussed, was the equivalent of Jonah letting Nineveh know they had about six weeks left. Both prophets extensively warned the people that God was fed up with their ways.

Possibly the saddest verses in the Bible are found in Jeremiah. Whereas Moses intervened on behalf of the people when God wanted to destroy them, Jeremiah is told several times by

God, "Do not pray for these people. I'm not listening."

Jeremiah's seventh chapter is known as the "Temple Sermon." He started the discourse by telling the people of Judah to change their ways if they wanted to keep living where they were living. He then asked them if they actually thought they could steal, murder, commit adultery, lie, practice idolatry and then go to church and believe everything was fine as if God could not see beyond the walls of the temple. In the 12th verse He tells them to remember what happened at Shiloh.

God instructed Jeremiah to deliver the warning but knew the people would not pay attention to it. He had already determined to boot Israel out of the Promised Land when He told Jeremiah to quit praying for them. God was right. The people made fun of Jeremiah, and politically well placed and influential prophets and priests branded him a false prophet.

Even after Babylon captured the leadership and wealthy people of Israel and looted the treasures of the temple, false prophets continued to preach that everything was fine. Jeremiah continued to preach repentance letting the people know that they had an opportunity to escape judgment. In the end, Jeremiah was the only person of any significance that was not taken into captivity.

America

Just as surely as God judged the nation of Israel, He will judge America. How far will our nation push before God regrets his protection and blessing? How loud is the cry already ringing in His ears arising from our land?

Just prior to the flood, God warned that He would not put up with man's wickedness indefinitely. God doesn't change, and obviously, neither does mankind. Early man rode donkeys, modern men ride in airplanes, but the donkey was never important. We marvel at the technological achievements of the modern age, but it was the heart of the man riding the donkey that was always the issue for God.

The hearts of Americans are every bit as obstinate as those of the nation of Israel which God marveled at in Ezekiel 16 over two and a half millennia ago. God's standards have not changed. He was enlightened long before the "Age of Enlightenment." The only thing the modern age has done for man is to provide fancier and more complicated ways to sin. Many Americans think that if the majority agrees and the law makes it legal, then it must be OK with God too.

But God has been dealing with man for thousands of years. To Him, the United States is just another arrogant blip on the radar. His principles are the same for all people of all epochs. Follow Him, receive a blessing; rebel against Him, be removed. There are countless examples in scripture of these principles at work through the ages: fertile land becoming parched, wealthy nations becoming impoverished, powerful nations destroyed.

The United States is suffering from a severe case of spiritual cancer. God is an impeccable spiritual cancer surgeon. The question remains, however, can the patient be saved? The next step in America's history may well be God drawing the line. When He does, it will not be a gradual demise that can be explained away. For such a feat, He demands the credit. America's judgment will be relatively quick.

When David sinned against God by taking a census that he had not been instructed to take and commanded his senior general to include everyone, though it was a sin to include the tribe of Levi in a census, God responded by offering David a choice of punishments. The first choice was three years of drought in which there would not be enough food. The second choice was three months of constant military defeats. The last choice was a disease that would overtake the nation for three days. If God has given the president a choice of judgments, he has not told the people yet.

How can I judge thee? Let me count the ways. There is a variety of ways that America could be destroyed that the government would be powerless to stop. God is in total control of nature, for example, despite what some egotistical self-proclaimed experts might say. Even they are fully aware of natural phenomena capable of destroying the entire planet.

Even within nature there are many possible avenues of judgment.

Volcanoes have throughout history destroyed cities and regions. The city of Pompeii which we know to have practiced every type of sexual perversion was destroyed by the volcano Mt. Vesuvius in the first century. Archeologists have found evidence of a volcano like occurrence that could possibly account for the destruction of Sodom.

Under Yellowstone National Park in Wyoming, a super volcano is brooding. In the past, it has erupted about every 700,000 years. The time is presently right for another eruption. Parenthetically, 700 millennia make modern America's one quarter of a millennium seem insignificant. The caldera or mouth of the Yellowstone volcano is approximately 34 by 45 miles. Compare that to the caldera of Vesuvius which is less than 1500 feet across and Mt. St. Helens which is about 6000 feet across.

Scientists say that when Yellowstone blows it could potentially cover three states with lava and most of the country with ash. Some predict that enough material will be released into the atmosphere to block sunlight for more than a year, triggering another ice age and effectively ending all life on the planet. A full blown Yellowstone eruption is not needed to bring judgment to America. God's hand may already be on the trigger of an eruption just large enough to do the job.

Every celestial body in our solar system gets pounded with asteroids. Earth is no exception. Since most asteroids impact the earth in the ocean and remote areas, estimates vary from one to ten years on the frequency of an impact at least equivalent to the atom bombs that were dropped on Japan at the close of World War II. There is archaeological evidence of as many as 60 impacts with a force of ten million megatons of TNT or greater. Several meteor craters visible by satellite measure in the neighborhood of 100 miles across. Many scientists believe that the moon was formed as the result of an asteroid collision with the earth.

Asteroids enter the earth's atmosphere every day. Most burn up before ever reaching the surface: the larger the asteroid, the larger the piece that survives the trip through the atmosphere and impacts the surface. Scientists have warned of many different consequences if a large enough asteroid hits the planet. The impact could kick up enough dust into the air to block out the sun and trigger another ice age. It could also knock the earth out of its orbit with dire consequences for life on the planet. Some have suggested that a large enough asteroid impact could destroy the earth's magnetic field and destroy all modern electronics.

As He showed in Egypt long ago, God is able to direct an asteroid, or a handful of asteroids, just large enough and precisely aimed to bring judgment to America without destroying the rest of the world.

Every so often, a new disease unleashes itself on the world. In the mid-14th century, the Black Death arrived in Italy aboard ships from Asia. Before it subsided after roughly one year, one third to one half of the population of Europe was dead. Even today, there is debate among scientists as to what disease was responsible.

In recent times, SARS, AIDS, West Nile Virus, Chikungunya and others have appeared and ravaged before being brought under control. New viruses have been discovered in previously frozen glaciers. Chikungunya, a previously unheard of African disease carried by mosquitos that causes its victims to fold up like a pretzel, infected 100,000 people in the Caribbean the first year it showed up there. Within five months of being discovered in the western hemisphere it had spread to 14 countries including the United States and infected a quarter of a million people.

Diseases, especially viruses, are also turning out to be smarter than expected. The flu virus, which after hundreds of millions of victims holds the record for number of people killed, mutates every year. One variant, the Spanish Flu, killed almost five percent of the world population in the early 20th century. Ebola has been around for centuries but also has the ability to mutate. When a virus mutates, the treatments that were formerly effective may no longer work. That is the reason a new flu shot is required every year. Some diseases that were not a major menace a few years ago have become more seriously threatening since they have developed a resistance to the antibiotics that are used to treat them.

Scientists believe there are millions of viruses in existence. Of those, only a couple of thousand have been classified. Some affect only plant life, some affect animals, and some affect people. Of the thousands of viruses classified, vaccines have been developed for just over a dozen. Viruses have their own DNA or RNA. They are so small they can only be seen with an electron microscope. When they come into contact with a cell of an infected host, they inject their own DNA or RNA into the cell, effectively hijacking that cell's function. The host cell then multiplies the virus and subsequently explodes in death, releasing more of the virus into the host's body to repeat the process with more cells.

When a person becomes sick enough from the virus to show symptoms, it has spread throughout the body enough to be present in exhaled vapor and also in any other bodily fluids. At that point, the virus can make the jump to the next person. Some viruses make the jump via transportation by insects such as ticks, fleas, and mosquitos.

Perhaps judgment in America will come in the form of some undiscovered microbe or bacteria or a new mutation of an old friend like the Flu virus or a stronger version of a recent invader like the Ebola virus. Judgment in the form of disease can be more refined. During the Black Death, there were pockets on the European continent that were never infected for some unknown reason though the disease reached to the most remote edges of the landmass.

Another option for God to bring judgment to America is the way He brought judgment to Judah at the time of Ezekiel and Jeremiah: a violent overthrow of the nation by an outside power.

Even after God relented from the catastrophe He intended to make of Ahab, Ahab continued to turn away from following God. In 1st Kings 22 Ahab invited Jehoshaphat, the king of Judah, to join him in a war against the Arameans. He had hundreds of prophets telling him it was a good idea, but Jehoshaphat wanted to hear from a true prophet, a prophet of the Lord. Ahab reluctantly sent for Micah.

Micah told Ahab that God was planning to kill

him and had sent a spirit of deception to deceive his trusted prophets and lead him into disaster. Ahab ignored Micah's warning and went to war in spite of it. The war abruptly ended when Ahab was killed in the battle.

The leadership in America has strayed from its founding principles and paid attention to deceitful prophets. Once strong spiritually and physically, the nation now languishes in the mire of spiritual decay and has grown weak economically and physically.

Some of our strongest, most determined and sworn enemies routinely steal our cutting edge technology. Our most dedicated and resolute ideological enemies are living within our borders, militant organizations that have clearly stated their intentions to physically attack us.

James said that a double-minded man is unstable in everything he does. A double-minded nation can be no different. America is more polarized than ever. The tension has become an obvious struggle between the poor, struggling to get by, and the rich; between those trying to please God and those wanting to have nothing to do with Him. And those in leadership selfishly try to please the majority in order that they may hang on to their power.

Perhaps when God draws the line it will be with a violent overthrow of our government by a nation fed up with our interference in their affairs such as China or Russia. Perhaps it will be a violent revolution brought on by a Muslim Jihadist group from a nation sick and tired of receiving our exports of moral filth. America, after all, is not content to welcome homosexual behavior within her own borders; she must use her financial wealth to blackmail or her military super-weapons to intimidate the rest of the world into following suit. There are nations and ideologies, however, that can't be bought and won't be intimidated.

America antagonizes and throws her weight around the world as if she were the only nation that mattered. In the early 60's when Russia planned to move missiles onto our doorstep, America mobilized to go to war. Yet, more recently, America had no qualms about placing more powerful missiles on Russia's doorstep. That is only one example of her double standard to which the world is not blind.

God has blessed America on a national level for centuries. Our armies have prevailed, and our security has always been sure. But America is turning away from God and becoming more blatant in its perversion. If things continue the way they are going, the time is short before God removes the blessing, and our armies will be decimated by the enemy.

The warning is clear in Leviticus 18. Practice the mentioned abominations and be thrown out of the land as the Native Americans were forced out of their land before us. God is not now, nor has He ever been, a respecter of individuals. He doesn't snap to attention for the president of the United States any more than He is flustered by the presence of any king, past or present. Ahaziah painfully learned that lesson as related in the opening verses of the book of 2nd Kings. God is not impressed by the power, prestige, or knowledge of any man. The only one God has any regard for is the man who is humble before Him and who practices true justice and mercy.

Repentance

Another possibility of what could happen next is repentance on a national level. It has happened before in America. Just prior to the revolutionary war in a period known as the First Great Awakening, repentance and revival swept through the land led by evangelists such as Jonathan Edwards and George Whitefield. Ideas such as temperance, women's rights, and the abolition of slavery came to the forefront during the Second Great Awakening which was significantly strong in the northeast part of the nation during the first half of the nineteenth century.

God's response to sin and repentance is illustrated over and over in the Bible. During the exodus from Egypt, for instance, the people became discouraged with how long it was taking to get to the Promised Land and rebelled against God and Moses. Numbers 21 says that God responded to their dissention by sending deadly poisonous snakes that inflicted severely painful bites. As death spread across the multitude, the people quickly repented for their defiance and asked Moses to intercede for them with God. When God saw their change of heart, He told Moses to make an image of a snake and raise it high on a pole so the people who were bitten could see it. Anyone who was bitten and looked at the serpent on the pole lived. God intervened because of the people's repentance, but the faith of the individual who was bitten was necessary for that particular person to escape the judgment. It is important to realize that God's invitation to deliverance was open to all. Incidentally, the image of a snake wrapped around a pole has become a universal symbol for medical practice.

God made a promise to Solomon after the temple was dedicated. He said that whenever He executed judgment against His people, whether it is in the form of a drought, or a swarm of locusts which destroy the vegetation, or a deadly disease sent to decimate the population, if His people would ask for forgiveness, He would restore them. The phrase in 2nd Chronicles 7 which begins, "If My people who are called by My name," is often used in reference to revival. The context of the verse in scripture is restoration from judgment.

The details of the passage spell out the procedure of repentance and getting a reprieve from God's chastising.

The first step is humility. Simply put, God wants His people to stop pretending to be little gods. They must realize and admit that He alone is God, and He alone has all the answers and has everything figured out. After the line is drawn, He has no patience for our inflexibility when it comes to His leading.

The second step is to pray and seek God's face. The word used for prayer has the connotation of intercession. God wants His people to intercede on behalf of the nation, to pray for those who do not know how to pray or for those who may not even know God, yes, and even those who are hostile toward God. When someone is hostile toward God, there is frequently betrayal or hurt in their experience that all too often, unfortunately, can be traced back to a church or one of its professed members.

The Aramaic way of saying, "In my presence" is, "In my face." To seek the face of God means to seek His presence. We are always in God's presence physically. When the scripture talks about coming into the presence of God, it's referring to our attitude and spiritual condition. Since God cannot tolerate sin, rejecting sin is the only way to be in His presence. Once in His presence, we can begin to hear Him and benefit from His love, His discipline, and His direction for us.

The last step in the process of repentance is to actually refrain from the wicked acts which initially brought about the judgment. As Jeremiah warned in Jeremiah 7, simply acknowledging the evil and going to church and saying, "I'm sorry," is not sufficient. Taking corrective action is necessary to actually receive forgiveness. It involves a change in thinking from, "This act is OK" to, "This act grieves the heart of God and is therefore not OK."

America is presently in the position where repentance on a national scale is needed. It is the only way to turn back the inevitable and avoid destruction. There is too much corruption in the justice system from the highest levels of government to the lowest levels of enforcement. The entire system needs to change its focus. God expects true justice. The people in the nation who best understand mercy are those who need it and never get it from their fellow man. Most of the affluent in the nation don't need it, don't understand it, and don't give it. God expects us to be merciful.

Most of the people in America don't realize that the nation is hanging on by a thread. There are a few extremely wealthy individuals in America who are merciful and practice charity. Even though their charity often makes the news, they are not in a position to need positive publicity. They are, however, in a unique position to make a significant difference in the lives of countless poor and downtrodden individuals and families. It is perhaps for their sake that God has not already brought judgment.

The church as an institution has been in a steady state of decline for decades. This is both a reflection on the church, as an institution not meeting the needs of the people at large, and a reflection of the population turning away from seeking spiritual help. But the church, in reality, is not an institution. It is not the building and the staff inside.

The church is the body of Christ. It is a spiritual entity made up of believers in Jesus. And while many churches, perhaps the majority, go through the motions with hardly any spiritual life, there are God seeking, God fearing assemblies and organizations of believers that can be found practicing mercy and strengthening the hands of the poor. Perhaps it is for this remnant that God has not already executed judgment on America.

But the church has been in trouble for a long time as evidenced by the many denominations and the unwillingness of the fractured pieces to accept each other and work together. As recorded in John 17, the prayer Jesus prayed shortly before His crucifixion was focused on the unity of His followers. But unity among Christians depends finally on Christians. Yet, instead of increased unity among His people, there is more disunity today than ever. America leads the world in a splintered Christian church, perhaps due to the tendency to act as judges instead of ministers, or personal pride that refuses to acknowledge mistakes, or perhaps fueled by the "inalienable rights" of life, liberty, and the pursuit of happiness. The many divisions within the church is the result of believers acting as though the church is simply a human institution made up of buildings, bylaws and a peculiar set of teachings.

The institution is only a tool in the work of equipping, and supporting one another as all follow Christ in the same spirit of humility and self-sacrificing love. Understanding that premise and the changing of hearts and minds is another important step toward national repentance. To put John's question in 1st John 4 another way, how can Christians hope to humble themselves before God and come into His presence when they cannot humble themselves before each other and tolerate each other's presence?

When the Spirit of God moves, revival is far more infectious than any virus. But repentance and revival cannot happen unless it begins with those who already have the Spirit. The church in America needs to change its focus from seeking political and earthly power to seeking the power of God. It needs to change its goal of pleasing the people to pleasing Him. It needs to cease worrying about numbers and offerings and begin to worry about His presence and His blessings.

Or, the people of God in America can accept the status quo and go along with the political tide and be swept away with the rest of the nation when judgment comes.

Possibly the harshest rebuke Jesus gave to the established religious order in His time can be found in Matthew 23. He called the religious leaders snakes and said they regularly practiced extortion and lived for their own pleasure. After He pronounced a curse on them he lamented the state of Jerusalem. He said He wanted to protect the people as a hen protects her baby chicks, but the people wanted to go their own way. Within 40 years of His pronouncement, Jerusalem was reduced to rubble by an invading army.

"I have fought the good fight, I have finished the race, I have kept the faith; the Righteous Judge will receive me and all who love His presence with a crown already set aside"

- Paul – 2Timothy 4:7-8

CONCLUSION

Let the Bible Speak for Itself.

The Bible is the most researched and critically evaluated book of all time. No other ancient text has been researched and examined to the degree that the Bible has in order to be as certain as possible concerning the accuracy of what the original authors penned.

At the conclusion of the first chapter in his second letter, Peter says that we are not following cleverly fabricated fairytales but the accounts of eye witnesses. He goes on to say that we would do well to follow the confirmed prophetic word. But he warns that the words of scripture are not the product of any man's will nor are they meant to be privately interpreted. So even though the many translations differ in the exact words they choose to translate the texts from Aramaic and Greek into English, they are all trying to convey the particular meaning of the original text.

The Bible is freely available through many churches and organizations that give them away to anyone wanting a copy. It is also freely available via the Internet in many translations as well as in Greek and Aramaic.

Having multiple translations is much better than having a single translation when trying to understand a complicated passage such as Romans 3:25. Hardly any two English translations are the same. On the other hand, a simple and straight forward verse such as John 11:35 is translated using the same words by most of the English translations. "Jesus wept." Translations don't change words for the sake of being different. Otherwise you would expect to find, "Jesus cried," or "Jesus shed tears," both legitimate translations of John 11:35.

Experience is a dependable teacher for those who receive its instruction. We apply what we learn through experience to similar situations we face later. Since we learn through experience, it is also common for us to project our feelings, thoughts, and beliefs on other people before we really know them. We can even gain a limited understanding about God based on what we know about our character. As a parent, we get a hint of how God feels toward us. But no man is capable of fully understanding the depths and wisdom of God.

A wise Christian will let the Bible inform his experiences and opinions instead of letting his experiences and opinions change what the Bible says. Passages of scripture, taken in context, are confirmed by other passages of scripture. If two passages of scripture seem to contradict each other, the flaw is likely to be either in the interpretation or in the fact that too little is known about the subject. God has established a pattern of giving individuals as much as they need instead of all that they want. He is God and has everything well in hand; we do not need to know everything, though it is human nature to want to.

It is a perilous mistake to believe that since God is love, He wouldn't judge or condemn anyone. Such a belief arises both out of a misunderstanding of love and a lack of understanding of the scope of God's commitment. The rationale, "If I loved someone then I would (or wouldn't); therefore God..." is inherently flawed. First of all, I am not God and secondly, I do not see the whole picture. God not only sees the circumstances, He reads the heart of the individual and understands the ramifications of His will to all who are involved, presently and in the future, in every decision He makes.

Too often, scripture is morphed into a politically correct or religiously correct interpretation as Paul warned against in the beginning of the 4th chapter of his second letter to Timothy. The danger in changing what a passage in scripture says is twofold. First, what the passage is actually trying to say is lost. Second, the morphed, politically correct version teaches error. An excellent example is the passage from 1st Peter referred to earlier in the section on marriage. Many English versions today translate "weaker vessel" as "weaker sex" or some variant thereof to imply that the wife is weaker in certain ways.

The Greek in 1st Peter 3:7 explicitly includes the adverb *hōs* which means "as", "like", or "in the same manner". A few English versions translate the passage literally, "give honor to your wife in the same manner you honor a weaker vessel." Several other versions interpret the passage instead of translating it and convey as gently as possible that the wife is weaker. One particular previously literal translation changed its wording in the most recent editions from the former phrasing to the latter.

Several decades ago, popular feminists garnered attention when they took issue with this verse as rendered in several versions, and rightly so. The Greek text makes no reference at all to a "weaker sex", a "weaker partner", a "weaker nature", or a "weaker person." In fact, the wife may be stronger than her husband in many ways. Peter is not making a statement about the wife's strength or women's strength in general. The wife's strength is completely beside the point. His instruction most certainly holds for husbands who are weaker than their wives.

One of the goals of every Christian should be to seek and live by the truth. That begins with accepting the scripture, unvarnished, for what it says. Seeking understanding of the scripture is step two. Changing what the scripture says to accommodate one's beliefs is a step in the wrong direction.

Confusion on What the Bible Says About Homosexuality

Most Christians have never seriously studied

the subject of homosexuality from the scriptures and are subsequently taken in by the volume of prevalent false teachings. Homosexuality, as a specific perversion of God's intentions, has been around about as long as the Bible itself.

Confusion begins when the liar comes and says, "Did God really mean what you think He said? Let's think this through." The liar wins when Christians put their Bible down or try to diminish or explain away what it teaches.

In this day and age it is popular for nonbelievers to ridicule Christians for their beliefs, practices, and attitudes. Sincere Christians become confused when they cannot distinguish between ridicule that is justified and ridicule that arises out of ignorance. Justified ridicule was anticipated in the New Testament. Hence, it warns us against suffering as an evil doer. When Christians fail to abide by God's direction, they not only bring ridicule upon themselves, they impair the ministry of the church as a whole.

Compounding the problem of confusion among Christians is the prevalence of what Jesus called wolves with insatiable cravings which to all outward appearances look like sheep. A more current analogy is the fox guarding the chickens in the hen house. Scripture uses a variety of pictures to illustrate the difference between the godly and the godless. The godly are spiritually alive, radiate light, live in peace and serve others selflessly, while the godless are spiritually dead, conceal their motives and actions in darkness, stir up conflict and make sure their own desires are met.

The Bible is clear in what it says about homosexual behavior. God hates it, He will not long tolerate it, and those who encourage it are perverse. There is no confusion within the scripture on the subject.

One way to address the confusion regarding how the scripture deals with homosexual behavior is to realize that God's love is expressed through discipline as well as through blessing. Out of love He warns us against the abominable. This is no different than parents who would warn their young child to stay away from a hot stove top or electric outlets; situations which are beyond the child's understanding but are dangerous nevertheless. The child that trusts his parent will avoid possible injury, while the stubborn child may regretfully learn for himself the wisdom in the parent's warning.

Almost half the references to discipline found in the Bible are found in the book of Proverbs which also contains one in four of the scriptural references to wisdom. Proverbs correlates wisdom and discipline frequently, but in the 12th chapter, Solomon comes right out and declares that a person who hates to be corrected is stupid. Human nature resists discipline and wants to be right all the time. This works in the liar's favor as he tries to create confusion within the heart of the Christian. A wise Christian has learned to appreciate discipline.

A young father was walking with his 5-year-old son through a field near a pond. Suddenly he sternly shouted, "Stop!" The boy uncharacteristically stopped without taking another step. There was no time to explain the situation or why there was sudden danger to the boy. The father had seen a very large snake crossing their path only a couple of feet in front of them and out of love barked the terse command to his son. Whether it was the wisdom of discipline or the assurance of his father's love, the young lad saved himself from possible harm through his unquestioning obedience.

There are several passages of scripture that convey an understanding of God's hatred of and warnings against homosexual behavior. Other passages contain mere terse commands. Our knowledge of God's nature and His love for us should be all that we need to follow His direction without question.

In the first half of John 10, Jesus draws a distinction between Himself, the good shepherd, and the thief who sneaks into the sheepfold. In that passage, Jesus said that the thief's only purpose among the sheep is to kill, steal, and destroy. On the other hand, He declared that His purpose was to bring life. The source of any teaching can be judged by the ultimate results it brings. The enemy's deception will eventually become obvious through the ensuing consequences. Scripture specifically lists homosexual behavior as one of the things which leads to disaster.

The Role of Fear in Christian Attitudes

Some Christians have an irrational fear that homosexuality is somehow contagious and can practically be transmitted through physical contact or close proximity. Out of that fear, some of them have gone so far as to take their children out of organizations where they discovered that the leadership condoned or practiced homosexuality. Those types of actions are in fact underhanded condemnations which result in resentment and pain in the hearts of the very ones Christians are called to love and minister to.

Paul assures us in 1Corinthians 15 that bad company corrupts good morals. Nevertheless, a child's parents are the strongest influence on his character and belief system. A gem of wisdom from Proverbs 22 explains that the values and beliefs children learn from their parents will stick with them the rest of their lives. There are no perfect teachers or leaders in youth organizations, not even in the church. All people struggle with sin in one form or another, some forms more obvious than others.

Unless we turn into hermits and live cut off from the world, coming in contact with sin is inevitable. Throughout the land, there are many who reject godly values and are not ashamed to let everyone know about it. There are individuals who have the eradication of godly values as their personal mission in life. Fear of inadequacy is a natural response when trying to relate to someone who may seem to have a better working knowledge of the Bible while rejecting all that it says. But nowhere in scripture does it say that Christians are adequate by themselves.

The truth remains; when dealing with other's hearts, a Christian is only an instrument in the hand of God. Apart from prayer, acting out of love and telling the truth in humility, without condemnation or rejection, is the extent of our responsibility and power. God deals directly with the spirits of men and uses our obedience to accomplish His purpose in the hearts of those individuals He has placed in our path. Understanding that we are not responsible for the results of our testimony should dispel a certain amount of fear.

We should not fear our inadequacy knowing that God accomplishes His will through us in spite of our insufficiency. The ability to be light and salt flows like water from the presence and power of the Holy Spirit which resides within a Christian. When Jesus told His followers that they were the light of the world, He meant that men would seek them out for guidance. When He told them in the same message that they were the salt of the earth, He meant that men would be hungry for what they had.

Fear is the enemy's go-to tool to hide the light and mask the flavor of the salt. A Christian who is living in fear is not free to hear, much less follow, the prompting of the Holy Spirit. Fear closes the door to the blessing of God. As a result, he essentially becomes ineffective at being a channel of God's ministry. Hebrews 2 tells us specifically that Jesus came in the flesh to destroy the one who had the power of death and used the fear of death to enslave the world's population.

While trying to speak the truth, self-consciousness easily traps Christians and kindles fear. How do I look, am I important, what will people think of me? But the love and truth we share is not based on anything within us. When we lose focus of God's direction and turn our concentration inward, we cease being a conduit of His ministry. A simple rule of thumb to remember is: focus on self gives rise to fear, focus on others leads to ministry.

Fear and doubt also pervert a Christian's perspective. Doubt asks questions such as, "Can a homosexual be delivered?" A Christian should always strive to have the viewpoint of faith. The viewpoint of faith transforms the question and makes it rhetorical. "Can God free a homosexual?" The simple answer to that question is that God can do whatever He wants to do. Believing in the power and love of God is an important key to faith.

Ministry to a self-confessed homosexual should be no more fearful than ministry to a self-confessed liar or ministry to a self-confessed thief or ministry to someone with any other problem. After all, ministry is basically meeting a person's needs. The person doesn't have to articulate or even be aware of his need for ministry to happen. Sin is often the result of a person trying to meet his own needs in an inappropriate or ungodly way.

Ministry cannot happen unless the person is willing to receive it, no matter how clearly one understands the problem or the solution. No one in need of help can be forced to accept it. No amount of reasoning or arguing will change that. Trying to force ministry does more harm than good.

When a Christian acts in confidence instead of fear, the chances of being able to help others increases. Fearless ministry to one who practices homosexual behavior is summed up in Micah 6:8.

First of all, be fair. Show respect since all men are equal before God. Secondly, be merciful. It is likely that they have already been preached at to the point that they are no longer listening. Teddy Roosevelt once observed, "No one cares how much you know, until they know how much you care." Ministry is not parroting the truth; it is the result of compassion enabled by the Spirit of God.

The Role of Prejudice in Christian Attitudes

It is important for a Christian to realize that people are people regardless of their beliefs, political leanings, or labels that they wear. God has called every Christian to fulfill the promise He made to Abraham; to bless the world through Christ. That is the big picture.

Pride, anger, sloth, gluttony, and other sins are not a matter of ethnicity, gender or race, but a consequence of the condition of the human soul. Social norms are a matter of conditioning and are also not dependent on gender, race or ethnicity.

People are social creatures and are comfortable in groups, but they seem to always form exclusionary groups. This fact has become evident in the church over the centuries through the formation of denominations in contrast to the Jesus' longing which was articulated in His prayer recorded in the final chapters of John. Not only has there been the continuous dividing of the church into denominations, churches split within a denomination. Even since New Testament times, factions have been known to develop within individual congregations.

People seem to be comfortable with defining their group by who doesn't belong. They want to know who "us" refers to and who "them" refers to. Then of course, those that don't belong form their own exclusionary group. With little congenial contact between groups, misinformation multiplies. That, plus an absence of even the motivation for understanding, leads to prejudice.

Once people are labeled as homosexual, many Christians erroneously associate them with some sort of preconceived "homosexual" group. Without any further knowledge about them, all kinds of assumptions are made about their background, motivation, lifestyle, habits, personality and more. In addition, most Christians place homosexuals outside their own group. They, by definition, do not belong.

But those who practice homosexual acts are first people with their own histories, hurts, motivations, and problems. Prejudging someone inflicts pain and causes the person to feel helpless and small and precludes the possibility of any ministry. It also discounts the fact that Jesus gave His life for them.

Hatred Comes Easy to Mankind

Prejudice and fear often lead to hate which sets in motion hateful behavior. Over the centuries, the three most common differences which have formed the basis of prejudice and fear have been religious, racial, and economic status.

Historically, prejudice has escalated into full blown war. The crusades were a series of wars in the 11th century that the Christian church waged against Moslem held areas in Eastern Europe and the Middle East. The 30 years' war, which destroyed Europe in the first half of the 17th century, involved factions of the Christian church. Our own civil war, which decimated the southern half of the country, was essentially fought over the right to own Africans as slaves. In more modern times, Ireland became a war zone between wealthy and poor factions of Christians. The Middle East is constantly at war either between Jews and Muslims or between the various factions of Muslims.

Tolerance is a foreign concept for some who claim to be Christian. It seems to go against the principles of evangelism and holiness. How is it possible for a Christian to be holy and tolerant at the same time? Isn't holiness separation from the world and its practices? Does tolerance mean living cordially with the evil practices? Evangelism is changing the people in the world to bring them into salvation. But evangelism is only a tool in the hand of God.

Shouldn't a Christian strive to have God's perspective? He is most holy and hates sin to the point that He cannot tolerate its presence. Yet He accepted sinful man enough to share his flesh, walk among him, and die on a cross to save him. God makes a distinction between sin, which He hates, and the sinner, whom He loves. The purpose of the light and salt Jesus talked about is to attract those outside the church who are dying and don't realize the predicament they are in. Intolerance has the opposite effect in that it drives people away.

In Matthew 13, Jesus gave two perspectives on the kingdom of heaven. The first perspective is illustrated by the parable of the sower. In Jesus' explanation of the parable he makes several points. First of all, anyone can hear the word of the kingdom. That includes drunks, liars, adulterers, idolaters, murderers, and, yes, homosexuals. Another point of the parable of the sower is that the effect the Word of God has on an individual's life depends on how he receives it and responds.

The second perspective on the kingdom is found in the parable recorded in Matthew immediately after the parable of the sower. In the second parable, after the sower sowed his field with good seed, an enemy sowed the same field with tares. The enemy Jesus referred to is the same one Paul made clear in Ephesians 6: evil spiritual forces. Just as the good seed in the first parable was the word of the kingdom of God, the bad seed is the deception, temptation, and perversion from the enemy. The hearts of men decide which type of seed they receive and eventually bear the associated fruit of their choice.

The enemy in the second parable tried to destroy the crop of the sower. Man naturally reacts in anger and hatred in such circumstances. The servants wanted to immediately uproot the tares. The sower, in his wisdom, forbids his servants from pulling up the tares. He realizes the harm that could come to the wheat which to the untrained eye looks virtually identical to the tares.

The first parable demonstrates evangelism,

the second demonstrates tolerance. As servants of God, Christians should take to heart both parables. Only God can look into a man's heart and know what's inside. He has not delegated to us His responsibility as the Judge of men's souls. He has not set up some sort of spiritual police force, though some Christians believe they are lead investigators in charge of such a force.

Countless people, including some of those who practice homosexual acts, are living their lives looking like tares when in fact they believe in God in the deepest recesses of their heart, but they have been wounded by a church or perhaps by a well-meaning, intolerant Christian. Instead of active rebellion against God, they are prisoners of their own fear, hurt and bitterness and they long for deliverance.

It's too easy for a well-meaning Christian to meet a self-professed homosexual and jump to all kinds of erroneous conclusions. The resulting hatred does more damage than good. The target of the animosity may likely experience hurt and rejection. Other Christians who may be unseen witnesses to the hatred and not understand what is happening will draw wrong conclusions about the supposed Christian doing the ministry. Unbelievers who cannot comprehend what is happening may well infer that Christianity is a hateful religion that is best to be avoided.

In the parable, Jesus said that the tares will be separated out at the time of harvest, which for America may be sooner than we think.

Christians Should be About Ministry

It's a very small thing for God to intervene in

nature.   Nature is fully compliant.   It's an entirely different matter when it comes to intervening in the hearts of men.   Our preconceived ideas, tradition, and the complexities of the distracting circumstances of our lives make it exceedingly trying for God to direct us.   Just like the parable of the sower, the thorns that fill our lives make receiving the word of the kingdom difficult.

What is ministry?   Jesus summarized what ministry looks like at the conclusion of Matthew 25. The short glimpse of what sort of things God expects is set in the context of the judgment of God that will come to all mankind. Two parables depict the impending nature of judgment followed by a short discussion that reveals the basis of judgment.

The first parable in the chapter is the parable of the ten virgins.   Half were wise and had prepared to wait as long as it took for the bridegroom's appearance. Half were foolish and only prepared for his expected arrival time. In other words, they did just enough to get by. The bridegroom showed up while the foolish were gone making further preparations for his unexpected delay.   They showed up at the wedding hall late and were turned away at the door as strangers. Jesus concludes the parable with the warning that we do not know exactly when He will return.

The second parable is known as the parable of the talents. The modern meaning of the word "talent" actually derives from this parable. At the time Jesus told the parable, it meant nearly 100 pounds of silver. The parable is about a wealthy landowner who entrusted his wealth to his three servants during the time that he would be far away in another country. He distributed his wealth according to how he perceived their ability. One received five talents; one received two talents; the last received a single talent. It's important to understand that even a single talent was a considerable amount of money in that day. One talent was equivalent to 14½ years of laborer's wages or about a quarter million dollars today in America.

The servants that had received five talents and two talents invested the fortunes and both doubled the landowner's investment. The servant that received one talent hid the fortune out of fear. The landowner chastised him for failing to seek even a safe investment with a bank. That servant was punished for being useless. The lesson in the second parable is simple. God has equipped His people in every way to accomplish ministry free from fear. He has showered us with gifts that He fully expects us to use. He has even prepared the ministry for us to accomplish.

The last part of the chapter illustrates what ministry looks like. Jesus says that God will separate people on the Day of Judgment like a shepherd separates his sheep from his goats. On one side will be the people who fed the hungry they met, gave the thirsty they met something to drink, showed hospitality to the strangers they met, gave clothing to those they met in need of clothing, looked after those they knew were frail, and visited those they knew who were in jail or prison. On the other side will be the people who didn't do any of those things. The second group will be sent away for punishment while the first group will be rewarded as only God can reward.

To drive the point home, Jesus makes the ministry personal. He says, "I was hungry, I was thirsty." He explains that compassion and meeting the needs of others is equivalent in the eyes of God to meeting the needs of Jesus. People in Jesus' day were the same as people today, more likely to show compassion to an exalted individual they were trying to impress or trying to win favor from than to some poor beggar on the street.

Along with the lordship of Christ, this theme of serving the helpless is central to the New Testament. For example, Jesus illustrated what He called the greatest commandments with the parable of a random Samaritan. After the parable in which He compared the actions of the Samaritan with an indifferent Levite and an apathetic priest, He asked rhetorically which of the three proved to be a neighbor to the unfortunate victim of highway robbers.

Paul says in Ephesians 2 that we have been recreated by God as part of the body of Christ for the purpose of conducting the business of helping others as a lifestyle. God has already laid out the business for us to conduct.

Helping others with their most serious needs cannot be boiled down to a one size fits all system. Ministry is individual and personal. What meets a deep need in one person may not be helpful at all to another person with the same need. That is why prayer and sensitivity to Christ's leading are critical aspects of ministry.

All of Jesus' teaching points to the ministry of God. When the destitute cry out to God, He answers their prayer and uses His body as the primary means of provision. If the members of the body are unprepared or they're living in fear and hiding their talent, they fail to conduct the ministry God has arranged for them.

Helping someone is not equivalent to condoning their sin. When Jesus told the accusers of the woman caught in the act of adultery, "Let him who has no sin throw the first stone," He was not condoning her sin. He met her need because of her sin. If Christians only helped those without sin, no person would ever get help from a Christian. That is the ultimate perversion of what God intended.

Those who practice homosexual acts also get hungry and thirsty, suffer poverty and find themselves in hospitals and jails. Preaching to them or arguing about their understanding of the Bible or their sin is no way to meet their needs or show the love of Christ. Leave room for the Spirit of God to convict. They will come asking for direction when they are ready to trust you and God.

Paul argues in Romans 2 against judging others and reminds us that it is the goodness of God that leads us to repentance. That injunction against being judgmental of others includes self-professed homosexuals. In 1st Corinthians 9 Paul said he sympathized with all those he met in order to save some of them. He specifically listed the Jews, the lawless, and the weak; three groups of people that Christians in His day looked down upon. Interestingly, the word he used for "weak" is the same word Jesus used in Matthew 25 which is most frequently translated as "sick".

The Lord expects us to be prepared. Study the scripture prayerfully, seeking the heart of God. Don't waste precious time by sowing seeds of discontent. Exercise faith instead of succumbing to fear. The light and salt which emanate from God's nature within will draw those in darkness to you. We need to do our part as God directs knowing with confident assurance that God will do His part.

ABOUT THE AUTHOR

Richard Sones grew up as the eldest son of an Army Signal Corps officer and, as such, lived all over the world. Moving frequently, he attended army chapels and benefitted by learning under the guidance of chaplains from many different Christian denominations. After earning a Master's degree in Divinity, he was ordained as the pastor of a small, 150 year old Baptist church in rural Amelia County Virginia.

Having army blood in his veins, it wasn't long before he answered the call to duty and President George H. W. Bush commissioned him into the army as a chaplain.

While serving in uniform, Chaplain Sones had frequent opportunities to counsel gay service members and help them with their problems long before, "Don't ask, don't tell" became an issue. He counseled and assisted them without bias or censure and with the same degree of compassion as he had for all of his soldiers. He has long believed that people are people and is ever conscious of the paraphrase from John Bradford, "There but for the grace of God go I."

Now retired from the army after serving nearly 28 years, he continues in ministry as a hospital chaplain in El Paso, Texas where he lives with his wife of more than 35 years. His four children are grown and on their own adventures in life.

Richard enjoys teaching as much as any aspect of ministry. He has a heart and knack for taking complicated themes and making them easy to understand. Due largely to the leadership training he received over the course of his military career, he is adept at putting things in perspective, cutting through the fluff, and getting to the meat of a topic.